When Zarathustra Spoke

Bibliotheca Iranica
Zoroastrian Studies Series, No. 2

No. 1
Jean Kellens
Essays on Zarathustra and Zoroastrianism
Translated and Edited By
Prods Oktor Skjærvø

When
Zarathustra
Spoke

The Reformation of
Neolithic Culture and Religion

———————✦———————

Mary Settegast

Mazda Publishers Inc.
Costa Mesa, California · 2005

Mazda Publishers, Inc.
Academic publishers since 1980
P.O. Box 2603, Costa Mesa, California 92628 U.S.A.
www.mazdapub.com

Library of Congress Cataloging-in-Publication Data
Settegast, Mary.
When Zarathustra Spoke: The Reformation of Neolithic Culture and Religion
    p.cm.—(Bibliotheca Iranica: Zoroastrian Studies Series; No. 2)
    Includes bibliographical references and index.
        1. Zoroastrianism—History. 2. Zoroaster.
            3. Mediterranean Region—Antiquities.
        4. Middle East—Antiquities. I. Title. II. Series.

BL1572.S48   2005   295'.09—dc22   2005041707

ISBN: 1-56859-184-5
(case bound, acid-free paper)

Contents

Illustrations

Preface & Acknowledgments

I began studying the life and teachings of Zarathustra in New York City in the 1970s. At the time I was enrolled in the graduate school of archaeology at Columbia University, specializing in the Neolithic of the Near and Middle East. An earlier background in classical mythology was already directing my interest to the possibility of using references from ancient Greek and Roman literature, passages that modern scholars tended to dismiss as "mythic," to resolve some of the anomalies in Late Paleolithic and Neolithic archaeology. The product of that synthesis was the book *Plato Prehistorian: 10,000 to 5000 BC in Myth and Archaeology,* first published in 1986. In its final section I began to explore the possibility that the massive spread of farming after 6500 BC, which reformed and secured the Neolithic Revolution from Iran to the Aegean, might have been inspired by the teachings of Zarathustra, the Persian prophet whom several ancient Greek and Roman historians had placed in the last half of the seventh millennium BC.

In the twenty years since that book was completed, the archaeological picture has become much clearer and more detailed, and the correction or "calibration" of radiocarbon dating has been extended back through the Neolithic period. These advances have encouraged me to reopen and expand the investigation of the ancient dating of Zarathustra, particularly in light of recent innovations in the theoretical framework of Neolithic studies. In 1987 Colin Renfrew proposed a Near Eastern location and a Neolithic time frame for the original homeland of the Indo-European family of languages, to which the Iranian tongue (the language spoken by Zarathustra) belongs. A few years later Jacques Cauvin effectively argued for the influence of ideology on the origin and spread of farming, the defining Neolithic activity (and a religious imperative for Zarathustra's followers). Although the conclusions offered here differ substantially from the ones drawn by Renfrew and Cauvin, I am indebted to both men for providing the scholary foundation on which much of my argument rests.

I am also immensely grateful to the several archaeologists who read and commented on parts of the manuscript at various stages of its completion. The thoughtful reviewing by Constantinos Koutsadelis, Maud Lebreton, and Güner Coskunsu was invaluable, although their assistance should not be mistaken for an endorsement of my interpretation of the archaeological material. I owe thanks as well to David Harris and again to Colin Renfrew for the hospitality extended to me while I was in England, and to the staff of the archaeological library at University College, London, for allowing me the use of its considerable resources.

The importance of Jeff Fuller to the creation of this book cannot be overstated. As both editor and book designer, he has benignly influenced every aspect of the process — including the well-being of its grateful author. Our use of many of the illustrations that first appeared in *Plato Prehistorian* has allowed the artistry of Ann Hatfield, Eliza McFadden, and Elizabeth Wahle to be viewed again and their considerable talents to be appreciated in a new context.

While writing this book, I also received valuable suggestions from several friends who read all or parts of the emerging manuscript. The comments of William Irwin Thompson, Mark Ringer, Whitfield Reaves, Susan Edwards, Melanie Walker, Thea Tenenbaum, Rafaele Malferrari, and Suzanne Walker were extremely useful, and my heartfelt thanks goes to each of them. Of the many others who offered encouragement and suppport, I am particularly indebted to George Peters, Edna and Ruzwa Cooper, Ginny Threefoot, Carol Kobb — and above all, Don Copelin.

MS

Boulder, Colorado
settegast@earthlink.net

In memory of
Robert J. Braidwood

CHAPTER ONE

Neolithic Images

"The principal scientific advances are known to come not so
much from the linear accumulation of new facts but rather
from the periodic questioning of our least criticized premises."

— Jacques Cauvin,
The Birth of the Gods and the Origins of Agriculture

There is perhaps no more fascinating period in human history than the
one we call the Neolithic. Beginning around 9500 BC* in the Near East
and spreading to Europe and the Iranian plateau three thousand years
later, this "new stone" age becomes more genuinely mysterious with
each archaeological excavation. Widely associated today with the shift
from hunting and gathering to an agricultural economy, the Neolithic is
emerging as a time of social, technological, and religious innovation as
well. The immense changes that took place during the several phases of
this "Neolithic Revolution" have led prehistorians to compare its ultimate
impact to that of the Industrial Revolution, for it was Neolithic culture
that laid the foundations for urban civilization.

And yet the driving force behind these changes continues to elude
prehistorians. The more technically precise archaeology becomes, the
more complex Neolithic society is revealed to have been — and the less
adequate our theories of why it came into being. Each year we find the
archaeological reality moving farther away from the image, developed
in the early twentieth century, of primitive peoples huddled with wild
animals and plants into drought-formed oases and somehow emerging
with an agricultural way of life.

Calibrated radiocarbon dates, or their approximations, are used throughout this book.

We now know that as early as the eighth millennium BC, Neolithic peoples had designed elaborate ceremonial structures, developed pyro-technologies — including the production of lime plaster, often stained red or black, with which they covered floors, walls, and hearths of their substantial mud-brick buildings — and organized far-reaching networks of exchange for turquoise, obsidian, and raw copper. They were skilled mariners as well as farmers, and some of them are likely to have lived within a hierarchical or stratified society, as suggested by the size and complexity of the Neolithic settlement at Çatal (chá-tal) Höyük, an excavated portion of which is shown at figure 1.

Recognizing the mismatch between these new discoveries and the image of primitive villagers struggling to survive, one pair of archaeologists finds us now "at a stage when we should ignore all previous assessments in the course of reexamining the evidence and revising our perception of this key era of prehistory."[171] The call for reassessment is joined by a growing number of prehistorians who feel that a true understanding of the Neolithic will be achieved only when its belief systems are correctly deciphered and the influence of ideology on human choice — even in this early period — is recognized. Before exploring these new directions, it will be useful to look back briefly at the train of academic thought that left us with an image of the Neolithic that no longer fits the facts.

Early Misconceptions

Originally the term Neolithic was used by prehistorians in the late nineteenth century to mark a change in the way stone tools were crafted. No longer restricted to the Paleolithic ("old stone") technique of chipping, Neolithic man was adept at grinding and polishing as well. Early archaeologists, building their theories on the findings of only a few excavations, concluded that these new stone-working techniques came into being along with several other elements of human culture — permanent settlements, pottery, and the domestication ("the systematic selection and propagation")[155] of plants and animals. A date of perhaps 5000 BC was then considered a fair estimation for what was believed to be the simultaneous appearance of these various innovations, and by the middle of the twentieth century, prehistorians considered the Neolithic age as a

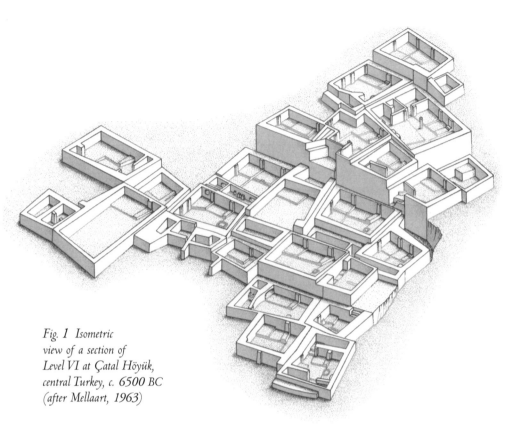

*Fig. 1 Isometric
view of a section of
Level VI at Çatal Höyük,
central Turkey, c. 6500 BC
(after Mellaart, 1963)*

whole to be rather well defined.

Their satisfaction was short-lived. Not only the time frame but the assumption that the Neolithic began with the simultaneous appearance of polished stone, permanent settlement, farming, and pottery began to unravel in the nineteen-fifties with the excavation of Jericho in the lower Jordan Valley. There a massive stone tower and wall dating from perhaps as early as 9000 BC was uncovered,[112] a structural complex that the excavator felt compared favorably to a medieval castle and which is still inadequately explained. Equally perplexing in terms of the existing Neolithic model was the discovery of what appeared to be a community of farmers within Jericho's walls — preceding the onset of pottery by some two thousand years.

The next "Neolithic" marker to fall was permanent settlement. In the nineteen-sixties, excavations at 'Ain Mallaha in the Jordan valley revealed a community of stone-based permanent dwellings dating to

c. 12,000 BC, several thousand years before the advent of the agricultural economy that was thought to have initiated settled life. The semi-sunken round houses at 'Ain Mallaha were accompanied by polished stone artifacts, but there was no evidence of domesticated plants or animals.[175]

When all of these supposedly Neolithic innovations did finally come together, it was in the context of communities like Çatal Höyük (fig. 1), where excavators have discovered — along with the presence of permanent dwellings, polished stone pieces, domesticated plants and animals, and pottery — a level of art, craft, and architectural achievement that once would have been considered impossible for the seventh millennium BC.

Acknowledging the obstacles to any wider definition, most archaeologists today use the term Neolithic simply to mean the change from hunting and gathering to an agricultural way of life. But rather than easing the task of the prehistorian, this narrowing of focus has accentuated an underlying lack of agreement about how agriculture began and, more importantly, why it spread.

The Domesticators

The warmer, wetter climate at the end of the glacial period (after c. 16,000 BC) allowed stands of the wild progenitors of wheat, rye, and barley to inhabit the Near East (defined by prehistorians as Israel, Jordan, Lebanon, Syria, and Turkey). Archaeologists often found these wild grains among the remains of plants gathered by the small groups of post-glacial hunting and gathering peoples who occupied these lands. But recent analyses of plant material from the site of Abu Hureyra suggest that those living along the Syrian Euphrates were actually cultivating einkorn wheat and rye as early as 10,500 BC. The same hunter-gatherers had earlier been consuming the wild forms of these grains, and analysts theorize that when the ensuing colder, drier climate (the Younger Dryas) caused the retreat of local wild stands in the eleventh millennium, seeds of these species were intentionally brought under cultivation.[98]

Others see the impact of the Younger Dryas on the steppe around Abu Hureyra as less critical, and inadequate to fully explain the origin of agriculture. Reversing the Marxist position — "from economy to ideology"—the eminent French archaeologist Jacques Cauvin has argued that in fact a "revolution of symbols" anticipated the establishment of a true agricultural economy in the ninth millennium.[39] In any event, domesticated plants represented only a small part of the multitude of species gathered and eaten by human beings for many centuries after their initial cultivation.

If the domestication of plants and animals was at first a gradual process, it began accelerating after 9000 BC, along with developments in the culture of the domesticators. The introduction of rectangular architecture c. 8700 BC in more northerly Near Eastern sites was approximately contemporary with the domestication of emmer wheat in the south; shortly thereafter barley, peas, lentils, and vetch were brought under cultivation as well.[6] By the middle of the eighth millennium, sheep, goats, pigs, and cattle were also domestic, and the advanced Neolithic society described in the opening pages was essentially complete. Its often-elaborate ceremonial complexes apparently served a belief system that was expressed through a particular reverence for cattle, an abundance of finely crafted arrow and spear heads, male statuary associated with the wild bull, and a "skull cult" suggesting the veneration of individual ancestors.[37]

The influence of these well-armed domesticators gradually spread through the Near East until c. 7000 BC, when cultural development slowed with the abandonment of a great many of the existing agricultural settlements. Although huge centers like Çatal Höyük continued to function until late in the seventh millennium, other, previously sedentary, peoples seem to have adopted nomadic ways of life.[189] Less than two thousand years after the agricultural impulse began to take form in the Near East, it appears to have been in danger of dying out.

The Potters

What happened next was not at all gradual. Around 6500 BC a multitude of new farming villages suddenly began springing up on virgin soil across the Middle East (Iran and Iraq) and into southeastern Europe, creating a vast network of agricultural communities with geometrically painted fine pottery and few, if any, traces of the weaponry, skulls, male statuary, and bulls' horns prized in the preceding period. After this late-seventh-millennium resurgence of the agricultural way of life, the future of farming was never again in doubt. Domestic grain and animals would soon reach Egypt, where they were as fundamental to the development of Egyptian civilization as they were to the first city states of Mesopotamia. As one archaeologist recently observed, "it is not so much the origins, but the spread, of farming that has had the major impact on human society."[181]

The reason for this immensely successful diffusion of the agricultural way of life remains a mystery. There is no evidence of the kind of population pressure in the seventh-millennium Near East that would require the colonizing of new and distant regions. Nor is there reason to believe that changes in climate had diminished traditional food sources of hunter-gatherers in the newly settled lands. On the contrary, after c. 6500 BC some or all of the basic complement of domesticated species that were cultivated or kept in earlier Near Eastern settlements (grains, pulses, legumes; sheep, goats, pigs, cattle) were introduced into very different—and often inhospitable—ecosystems from Turkmenistan and the Iranian plateau to the Mesopotamian lowlands and the high valleys of the Caucasus.

The date of c. 6500 BC also marks the approximate beginning of the "Neolithizing" of Europe with the spread of agriculture into Greece, and again we find no evidence of a climate-caused interruption of the abundance of wild foods exploited by the native population. A great deal of scholarly attention has been given to the question of whether the spread of farming to Greece also involved an influx of settlers from the Near East. As we will see, the majority of the new farmers were apparently indigenous peoples who voluntarily—and virtually overnight, relative to the process of domestication in the Near East—traded their hunting and gathering traditions for a fully agricultural life.

The question of why farming spread may then be rephrased: why would hunter-gatherers, whose way of life had served them well for tens of thousands of years, suddenly embrace so fundamental a change? They certainly could not have anticipated the far-reaching advantages farming might offer. Agriculture would seem to entail more actual labour, and if hunting and gathering peoples were not threatened by the depletion of their accustomed resources, which it seems they were not, then why indeed? With regard to the shift to farming in Europe, the prehistorian T. Douglas Price has observed that:

> "climate, environment, and population growth played a minor role, if any, in comparison to the changes that human groups chose with regard to their livelihood and way of life. In this context, the Neolithic Revolution probably had less to do with subsistence and technology and more to do with social and economic organization and ideology."[181]

The key word in that passage, for our purposes here, is *ideology*. The role of ideas and beliefs in changing the course of human history has recently been the focus of several important archaeological publications, of which perhaps the most influential is Jacques Cauvin's pivotal analysis in *The Birth of the Gods and the Origins of Agriculture*.[37] There he observes that for most of the twentieth century prehistorians accepted without question the view that major social and cultural changes originate in human biology — "our bodies and their need for food" — whereas a truly scientific approach would identify this view as simply another hypothesis to be examined. Cauvin further argues that the pervasive assumption that all major events in prehistory have an economic basis is actually a projection, back into the past, of our own materialistic obsessions. To treat this assumption as fact and automatically apply it to the interpretation of archaeological data is, in his view, unscientific in the extreme.

Thanks to Cauvin, Price, Ian Hodder,[99] and other prehistorians working today from similar premises, the focus of Neolithic studies seems to be shifting from subsistence strategies—what they ate — to the complex and symbolic nature of their ideologies—what they believed. We have observed that the ideology of the eighth millennium domesticators was expressed through a proliferation of "prestige" weaponry and displays of bulls' horns, human skulls, and male statuary. After 6500 BC, however, symbols painted on fine ceramics are almost the only clues we have to the beliefs held in the modest villages of the new epoch.

From Iran to Greece, this geometrically painted pottery quickly developed a remarkable technical and aesthetic refinement, with higher firing temperatures enabling potters to achieve vivid contrasts of dark and light in their patterns. While many of the fundamental motifs were held in common, each region also developed its own particular ceramic style. Overall, the care devoted to the crafting of fine pottery, which apparently was used for neither cooking nor storage, further contradicts the image of these new farmers as desperate peoples forced to adopt an agricultural way of life. They clearly — and from the vitality of their developed ceramic designs (fig. 2) one might even say exuberantly — chose to cultivate the earth.

To understand why, we are again encouraged to look beyond economic motivations to the ideological. Cauvin has in fact suggested

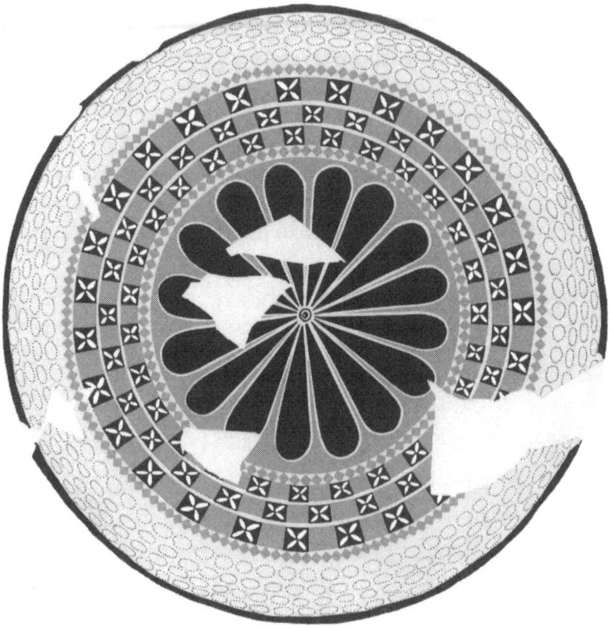

Fig. 2 Hand-built open bowl from sixth millennium Arpachiyah, northern Iraq. (after Mallowan and Rose, 1935)

that a new religion may have accompanied the spread of farming, "the one being the secret of the other."[37] The belief system he had in mind was that of the domesticators, whose agricultural settlements had earlier expanded in number over the course of the eighth millennium. But while the same domestic plants and animals then formed the core of the late-seventh-millennium painted pottery communities, the ceremonial structures and warrior-like symbolism of the original domesticators had all but vanished from these new villages. It is in fact the sudden change of cultural symbols accompanying the resurgence of agriculture after c. 6500 BC that suggests the presence of a new worldview, one perhaps powered by the "messianic self-confidence" that Cauvin found typical of the beginnings of the great expansionist movements of history.[37]

The Persian Prophet

We may never know with certainty what — or who — was responsible for this critical last phase of the Neolithic Revolution, but passages from the literature of antiquity could open a promising new field of inquiry. Ancient Greek and Roman historians ventured very few absolute dates in recounting events of great age, and yet several of them — Xanthus, Pliny, Eudoxus, Plutarch — individually and specifically gave dates ranging from 6500 to 6200 BC for the time of Zarathustra (Greek Zoroaster), the legendary Persian prophet whose missionary-borne message was said to have reached far beyond his native land.

Until quite recently, these ancient, almost mythic claims could neither be proved nor disproved. They have generally been ignored by both the Zoroastrian religion, which places its founder in the middle of the first millennium BC (c. 630 BC), and modern western scholars, who believe that Zarathustra is more likely to have lived in the second millennium BC (c. 1500-1200 BC). But the archaeological record of Iran offers little support for either of these conventional chronologies,[122] while, as noted above, there is considerable evidence of an ideological change accompanying the spread of agriculture after 6500 BC. Our comparison of the archaeology of the last half of the seventh millennium with texts from the oral tradition of ancient Persia (modern Iran) will further suggest that the leader of this new movement may indeed have been Zarathustra, living at precisely the time proffered by the Greek and Roman historians of antiquity.

The society the prophet set out to reform is believed to have been part of an archaic Indo-European tradition of nomadic or semi-nomadic pastoralists who revered individual ancestors, glorified their "warriors" (who were more likely to have been involved in cattle raids than in actual warfare), and worshipped a male warrior-god identified with the bull. Zarathustra apparently renounced the cult excesses of these lawless herdsmen, and Zoroastrian texts repeatedly emphasize the essential position of settled agriculture in the religious life — "He who cultivates grain, cultivates righteousness." (*Vendidad*, Fargard III.3.31)

In the course of his teachings, Zarathustra urged the individual men and women of his time to choose between *asha* (right order, truth, associated with light) and *drug* (bad or false order, deceit, darkness). The dualism for which the Zoroastrian religion is famous is believed by some interpreters to be rooted in the ongoing struggle between *asha* and *drug*, light and dark.[111] Precisely what action was to be taken by those choosing the path of *asha* is unclear in the *Gathas* (archaic hymns of unknown age that are believed to have been composed by the prophet himself), but many scholars believe that the primary struggle addressed by Zarathustra was between agricultural and nomadic ways of life. If the ancient historians were correct in placing him in the last half of the seventh millennium, the proliferation of new agricultural settlements after 6500 BC would suggest that the way of *asha* lay in cultivating the land — and that it was this choice, made again and again by individuals converted into this intensely missionary faith, that reformed and secured the Neolithic Revolution.

The historical impact of that choice — which led to the irreversible dominance of the agricultural way of life, attendant increases in population, and ultimately the development of cities — will be explored at the end of this investigation, as will the possibility that the teachings of Zarathustra profoundly influenced western religion and philosophy. Zoroastrian scholars claim that he was the first to give voice to ideas that later became articles of faith in Judaism, Christianity, and Islam. The belief in one supreme God, creator of the world, who is opposed by an evil power not within his control is fundamental to Zarathustra's teachings — as is the vision of a world moving toward a final state of perfection, an idea that has become embedded in the western psyche, fueling our linear sense of time and our faith in infinite progress.

The Scope of the Investigation

Before exploring further what is known of Zarathustra's life and teachings, I want first to briefly fill in the archaeological picture sketched above, reserving my interpretation of the excavated material until after the reader is better acquainted with Zoroastrian traditions. We will begin with the earliest permanent settlements in the Near East, c. 12,500 BC, and trace the prehistoric sequence through the beginning of an agricultural economy and, in greater detail, the weapons-rich culture of the domesticators. The apparent dissolution of this cultural tradition, or its dispersion into nomadic contexts, will bring us to 6500 BC and the new wave of agricultural settlements that began sweeping across Iran and Iraq at that time.

With the archaeological sequence somewhat secure, we will then take up the life and teachings of Zarathustra, followed by an exploration of the convergences between those teachings and the archaeology of the seventh millennium. The final chapters reverse this process. Instead of using Zoroastrian traditions to give meaning to Neolithic archaeology, we will rely on the archaeological findings to sort out some of the many gaps and discrepancies in the various accounts of Zarathustra's life. From its beginnings, Zoroastrian scholarship has had to contend with a lack of reliable information about even the most basic elements of his biography. When and where the prophet was born, where he found refuge after being cast out of his homeland, what the early communities of his followers were like, and what might his relationship have been to the Magi (whose order he is said to have founded) are all subjects of intense controversy. Essential to the resolution of each of these questions is the accurate dating of Zarathustra. If the ancient historians were correct in placing him between 6500 and 6200 BC, a coherent picture of his life — one requiring very little special pleading — should emerge from the archaeology of Neolithic Iran.

The perspective taken in this book is admittedly unconventional, and the congruences between late-seventh-millennium archaeological events and Zarathustra's teachings might be dismissed as nothing more than extraordinary coincidence were it not for the indications in the literature of antiquity. As we will see, these Greek and Roman historians lived in different centuries and used different points of reference in recording their not-quite-synchronous, late-seventh-millennium dates for Zarathustra. It therefore seems unlikely that they were borrowing from some common myth, or had accidently left off a zero in making their calculations, as some classicists have suggested.

Only recently have advances in archaeological techniques, including the calibration of carbon-14 readings, enabled us to judge the accuracy of these ancient claims and to give their authors a long-overdue day in court. What we find may confound the widely held view that the spread of farming must somehow be tied to the economics of survival. It may also challenge conventional datings of Zarathustra. But if there is any truth in the ancient claims, two of the great puzzles of prehistory — the late-seventh-millennium resurgence of agriculture and the placement in time of one of the world's most influential religious leaders — might be resolved as one. Modern translations of the *Gathas* have corrected Nietzsche's fabricated version of what Zarathustra said.[160] Let us see if modern archaeology can tell us when he spoke.

CHAPTER TWO

The Near East Before 6500 BC

"Cultures and civilizations rise and fall, some disappear altogether, blotted out from the face of the earth, but man, who made and unmade them, remains. Man does not disappear and although he may change his way of life, culture, religion, language... he cannot change his ancestors. All of us are descendants of Upper Palaeolithic Homo sapiens, or as it was put in a simpler age, the sons of Adam."

— James Mellaart, *The Neolithic of the Near East*

Before c. 12,500 BC the only occupants of the Near East were small groups of late Upper Paleolithic hunter-gatherers, perhaps one to five families, who changed the location of their campsites every few days or weeks. At some point midway in the thirteenth millennium, for reasons that remain unclear, clusters of semi-subterranean round houses — permanent settlements — began appearing in lands known today as Jordan, Israel, and Syria.

The new-stone techniques of grinding and polishing, from which the Neolithic originally took its name, were already known to these "Natufian" communities (named for the Wadi el-Natuf). At 'Ain Mallaha (map at fig. 5) these unexpectedly artistic people fashioned "decidedly elegant"[75] ground and polished stone bowls and plates, some with meander designs in relief (fig. 3). Natufian dead were often adorned with necklaces, bracelets, and dentalium-shell headdresses. While their toolkits continued to be dominated by the small chipped flints (microliths) known to the earlier inhabitants of this region,[228] bone sickles with carved animal heads (deer or gazelles) were new, apparently used to gather plant material.

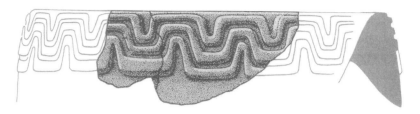

Fig. 3 *Rim of ground-stone bowl from the Natufian site of 'Ain Mallaha (after Perrot, 1966)*

Until recently, archaeologists had assumed that the grain being gathered was still in its wild form, but analysis of the excavated material from the settlement at Abu Hureyra in north-central Syria (map at fig. 5) has revealed the presence of domestic einkorn wheat and rye in Natufian levels, c. 10,500 BC.[98] At this time the people at Abu Hureyra were apparently enjoying an extremely diverse and nutritious diet; the remains of over 150 wild plants with edible seeds and fruit were found at the site, along with the bones of many different wild animals — gazelle, sheep, goat, aurochs cattle (*Bos primigenius*), deer, boar, turtles, and river fish among others. Only the dog was domestic.[6]

The next significant Near Eastern development — and one of the many unsolved mysteries of this period — was the sudden appearance of tanged arrowheads in the first half of the tenth millennium BC.

Fig. 4 *Khiam points (after Perrot, 1952; J. Cauvin, 2000a)*

The existing round-house architecture showed no change at this time, nor did hunters' practices or prey. Unable to find a more reasonable explanation for what he called a "spectacular development of projectile points," one prehistorian has suggested that they may have been used in warfare.[228] If so, the hostilities extended over a large portion of the Near East. The most widely dispersed of these weapons, called "Khiam" points (fig. 4) after the site of that name, are virtually identical in form from the Sinai desert to northern Syria.

In several sites the new arrowheads were accompanied by small figurines of women, bulls, and raptors (probably vultures, judging from later representations). Similar symbolic themes would continue to be expressed for several thousand years, prompting Cauvin's suggestion that this tenth-millennium "revolution of symbols" influenced the *page 5* development of settled agricultural villages in the following period.

Pre-Pottery Neolithic A, 9500-8700 BC

The decline of Khiam points marks the beginning of the cultural period archaeologists have designated Pre-Pottery Neolithic A (PPNA), a name that reflects the unexpected discovery that agricultural settlements predated the introduction of pottery by almost two thousand years (hence the "Pre-Pottery" Neolithic). At the PPNA site of Jericho (map at fig. 5), the massive stone wall and tower complex mentioned earlier was *page 3*

Fig. 5 Natufian, PPNA, PPNB sites mentioned in the text, 12,500 – 6500 BC.

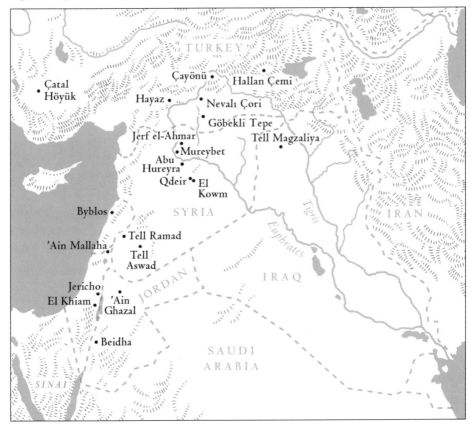

constructed around a community of round houses, now made of sun-dried mud bricks, a building material that is still used today in parts of the Near East. The purpose of Jericho's tower (fig. 6), which contained an interior staircase of hammer-dressed stone steps, remains essentially unknown; the wall is seen by some as a defensive structure, by others as a protection against flooding.[15]

Funerary rites at Jericho and elsewhere in this period included the occasional separation of skulls as well as "secondary" burials (the interrment of skeletons that had apparently been exposed elsewhere until clean). Cultural similarities among the various PPNA sites appear to have been limited, however, and the period from c. 9500 to 8500 BC has been described as one of "intense originality in which architectural solutions and subsistence strategies of amazing diversity coexisted."[37]

PPNA developments at round-house settlements on the Syrian Euphrates are exceptionally well-documented. Unlike the wall and tower at Jericho, the non-domestic structures at both Mureybet and Jerf el-Ahmar

Fig. 6 Artist's reconstruction of excavated portion (dark shading) of Jericho's tower and stone wall (after Kenyon, 1957, 1960)

(map at fig. 5) were large circular buildings whose interior benches suggest ceremonial or other community purposes.[209] Elsewhere at Mureybet two small buildings yielded traces of frescoes, the best preserved of which featured black, and perhaps also red, chevrons on a white background,[37] the earliest recorded examples of a tradition of wall painting that we will see carried to its furthest extreme at the seventh-millennium site of Çatal Höyük.

Although the inhabitants of Mureybet continued to harvest wild rather than domestic grain, the fishing that once was essential to Mureybet's economy almost disappeared c. 9000 BC, replaced by the hunting of large mammals and especially of cattle, the now-extinct wild aurochs. As Mureybet's excavator made clear, the new interest in the aurochs had nothing to do with the presence in the region of more cattle or fewer fish, but was rather a cultural preference.[37] His conclusion is supported by the presence of the horned skulls of wild bulls (bucrania) fixed to walls or embedded in benches at Mureybet and Jerf el-Ahmar.

Increasingly elaborate projectile points were now characteristic of almost all sites that earlier had known the Khiam point. These new weapons revealed an aesthetic component that Mureybet's excavator felt significantly exceeded the requirements of the hunt — and which anticipated an even greater elaboration of weapons in the years to come. Polished greenstone axes, another tradition with an immensely long life, were also introduced at this time. Of no apparent utilitarian value were the very small receptacles found at Mureybet, "little vases"[37] modelled in lightly baked clay that preceded the production of true pottery by two thousand years.

While these more northerly peoples of the Syrian Euphrates appear to have continued living as hunters and gatherers, settlers in Jordan and southern Syria were beginning to explore agricultural ways of life. Although grain had apparently been sporadically cultivated since the eleventh millennium, what Cauvin called an "agricultural economy"[39] was not achieved until the middle of the ninth. Between 9000 and 8500 BC, "the earliest systematic exploitation of domesticated cereals"[6] (emmer wheat) was recorded at the base level of Tell Aswad (map at fig. 5), a site near the modern city of Damascus. This region is believed to have been too dry to have supported wild wheat, and the plump, fully developed, domestic grains of emmer at Aswad indicated to archaeologists that the first settlers of the Damascus basin arrived already equipped with seed for planting.[6] Their origin is unknown.

Pre-Pottery Neolithic B, 8700-6500 BC

Although many of its main features were present earlier at Mureybet, the cultural period designated by archaeologists as Pre-Pottery Neolithic B (PPNB) does not officially begin until around 8700 BC with the introduction of rectangular architecture. Because the main focus of our investigation, the painted pottery cultures of c. 6500-6000 BC, emerged during the final stages of PPNB, we will look at this earlier Neolithic culture in some detail now and revisit it later.

Jacques Cauvin has identified four dominant characteristics of PPNB: rectangular architecture, finely crafted weaponry, the domestication of animals, and an emphasis on "symbols of virility," including male statuary associated with the bull.[37] Long blades struck from a boat-shaped ("naviform") flint core enabled the crafting of larger arrow, spear, and lance heads (fig. 7). A new type of retouch, long and shallow, was used on weapons at this stage and clearly represents more than a search for greater efficiency. But with little or no evidence of warfare during this period, excavators are puzzled by the care and attention that was given to the crafting of these weapons — particularly at a time when the hunting of wild animals was being replaced by the tending of domestic ones. At the eighth millennium PPNB settlement at Beidha in Jordan (map at fig. 5), almost 90% of the faunal remains were those of domestic goat, yet an astonishing variety of some twenty different types of arrow and lance heads was recorded at the site.[115]

The display of human skulls on the floors of houses and in ceremonial areas also reached its peak during this period, with lumps of clay occasionally used as pedestals to support and elevate the skulls. In an apparent attempt to recreate facial features, lime plaster was applied to the face and temples of several skulls at PPNB Jericho, with pieces of shell inserted for the eyes.[113] Prehistorians generally agree that these practices represent a form of ancestor worship. As one points out, the

Fig. 7 Examples of PPNB weaponry from Tell Aswad II, eighth millennium BC (after M-C. Cauvin, 1974)

careful preservation and display of skulls suggests that the memory of those individuals was intentionally maintained through ceremonial rites.[38]

In the eighth millennium, the large-scale manufacture of mud bricks in molds enabled the construction of multi-roomed rectangular houses, often densely packed within PPNB villages. Lime plaster was widely used in the laying of floors, often stained red or black and burnished to a hard shine. At sites in eastern Turkey, lime plaster occasionally served as a base for pavings of stone pebbles, creating a terrazo effect on the floors of structures that were apparently used for ritual activities.[170] Walls were often whitewashed, and floors were occasionally decorated with painted designs (e.g., a red sunburst on a black background at Abu Hureyra).[6]

Although PPNB settlement size ranged from large villages with populations numbering in the thousands to small bands engaged in a mobile, foraging way of life,[87] the material culture was marked by a high degree of homogeneity. Polished greenstone axes were ubiquitous, and the same crops were cultivated at PPNB settlements: emmer and einkorn wheat, barley, lentil, pea, flax. Whether these plants were all domesticated together in one place, or whether different species were taken into cultivation in different places, is unknown.[243] The same is true of the newly domesticated animals, which, by the middle of the PPNB period (c. 7500 BC), included cattle, sheep, goats, and pigs. A millennium later, some or all of the elements in this "Neolithic package" would be spread across Iran and west to Europe by the founders of the painted pottery communities that arose after 6500 BC.

PPNB Çayönü

While excavations of many PPNB settlements have yielded structures that apparently served religious purposes, the most clearly ceremonial are those found at sites in southeastern Turkey: Çayönü, Nevali Çori, Göbekli Tepe, and Hallan Çemi (map at fig. 5). The depth and richness of these ceremonial complexes establishes this region as what Cauvin called the "pre-eminent source of information on the domain of religion."[37]

Fig. 8   Foundation walls of a "grill plan" building at Çayönü, eighth millennium BC (after Redman, 1978)

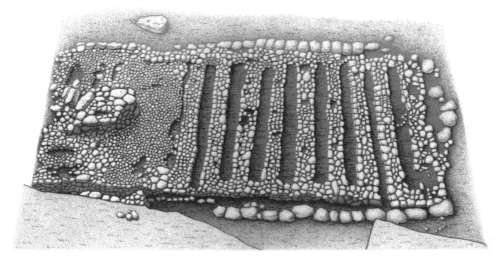

Of the sites named above, Çayönü offers both the most extensive excavation and the longest recorded sequence of settlements, with a base level that may predate even the early emergence of PPNB culture at Mureybet. Located near the headwaters of the Tigris river, Çayönü revealed an intriguing sequence of architectural styles or phases, from "channel plan" to "grill plan" (fig. 8) to "cell plan" to "large-room plan." Equally remarkable to archaeologists was the site-wide standardization within each of these architectural phases. In any given period, all of the domestic structures at Çayönü conformed exactly to the plan of that phase, with precisely similar distances between buildings. More puzzling still is the fact that whenever the settlement was rebuilt (numerous rebuildings typically took place within each phase), the orientation of each of the identical buildings was altered by exactly the same few degrees. Together with the extensive ritual activities undertaken at Çayönü (described below), these standardized building practices suggested to excavators that construction at Çayönü was "tightly controlled by a certain social class or group, possibly the spiritual leaders, who on certain occasions gave orders for abandoning the site and/or rebuilding it from one end to the other."[171]

The likelihood that a group of spiritual leaders directed important activities at Çayönü was enhanced by the discovery of three unique and patently non-domestic structures: the Flagstone, Terrazzo, and Skull buildings. The latter housed more than ninety human skulls within a context that provides perhaps the clearest evidence yet discovered of the use of Neolithic structures for ceremonial purposes. The added presence of horned aurochs skulls (one had been fixed to a wall facing the courtyard of the Skull Building) suggested to the excavators that a "bull cult" was celebrated at Çayönü in association with a cult of the dead.[168] More specific indications of ritual activities came from an altar-size slab of polished limestone that yielded samples of blood shown by hemoglobin crystallization tests to be compatible with that of humans. The blood of wild cattle was also identified on the slab and again on a black flint knife, some eight inches long, that was found on the premises. Analysts studying these remains have suggested that the Skull Building at Çayönü was used for some kind of ritual dismemberment as well as animal sacrifice.[237]

Polished greenstone axes (celts) and pestles were apparently sacred objects at Çayönü.[171] Some of the carefully sculpted stone pestles had been fashioned from broken celts and are believed to have been used, together with stone bowls, for the ritual preparation of food or drink. Of possible ceremonial use as well were small clay receptacles, primitive and lightly baked, with no more evident practical use than *page 17* the "little vases" found earlier at Mureybet.[168] The small female and animal figurines that were also made of clay at Çayönü may be less likely to have served ceremonial purposes, as they and their counterparts at 'Ain Ghazal and Nevali Çori were found only in areas of domestic occupation.[218]

Spread and Decline of PPNB

What Cauvin referred to as PPNB symbols of virility included male figurines (often ithyphallic) and the horn cores of the wild bull, as well as an abundance of elaborate weaponry. Given the reach of this culture into other lands, it is not surprising that he further described PPNB as "a conquering culture."[37]

Over the course of the eighth millennium, the Pre-Pottery Neolithic B culture expanded until ultimately its territory extended from southeast and central Turkey to southern Sinai and the Saudi Arabian desert. As we observed at Jericho, Beidha, and other PPNB sites in the south, an intensification of the crafting of ornate weaponry and the veneration of ancestors accompanied this cultural advance. PPNB influence may even have reached across the Iranian plateau and into the Indus valley. Although incompletely excavated, the Iranian sites of Zaghe and Sang-e Caxamaq reveal red-plastered floors and rectangular architecture,[158, 137] while recent excavations in Pakistan found domestic grain and rectangular structures at the eighth millennium site of Mehrgarh.[110, 18]

Shortly before 7000 BC, pottery entered the archeological record, appearing in several late PPNB sites in Syria, Turkey, and northern Iraq. Although its archaeological name was now inaccurate, the Pre-Pottery Neolithic B culture itself seems to have been unaffected by the advent of ceramic wares. Of the two different kinds of pottery that appeared almost simultaneously, one (known as "dark-faced burnished ware") was a grit-tempered, well-fired product (fig. 9) with burnished surfaces ranging in color from black to dark brown and gray.[62] Impressed decoration, sometimes made by a cardium shell, reinforced the resemblance of these Near Eastern ceramics to the "cardial impressed" pottery that was now appearing in cave sites elsewhere around the Mediterranean coast.[176] This is not the painted pottery of our investigation, and the provenance of these dark monochrome ceramics remains a mystery.

Fig. 9 Dark burnished ceramic bowl from Byblos (after Dunand, 1955)

The other pottery belonging to this period was chaff-tempered, soft, and rather crumbly. This technologically inferior product was often given a red wash or left cream-colored with a few lines painted in red below the rim.[37] As we will see in the following chapter, the transformation of this primitive "archaic ware" into painted ceramics of surpassing beauty is only one of the major cultural changes that occurred after 6500 BC.

Pottery failed to reach (or was rejected by) many PPNB settlements before their late-eighth or early-seventh millennium abandonment. In some of the PPNB communities that remained, signs of cultural disintegration are unmistakable. At Çayönü, for example, excavators found that the strict rules of standardization described above had been neglected in the last architectural subphase, as had the former homogeneity of plan, building technique, and structural orientation.[169] One of the long-maintained ritual areas, Çayönü's "Plaza," apparently lost its sacred function and was increasingly used as "an area for dumping garbage and for butchering."[171]

Evidence of cultural decline also appeared in Jordan at the huge PPNB site of 'Ain Ghazal (map at fig. 5), where reverence for ancestors, formerly expressed in skull preservation and the careful burial of particular individuals, apparently came to an end; skulls were no longer removed, and the dead were "crammed cheek-by-jowl in a single pit."[189] As significant, perhaps, were changes in the architectural layout, which suggested to excavators that part of 'Ain Ghazal's population was now practicing some form of nomadism.[204]

In fact, the abandonment of a good many PPNB settlements appears to have coincided with a general increase in nomadic herding or pastoralism.[37] As described by one archaeologist: "[Within] a period of but several hundred years, the fabric of life had gone from elaborate and large population aggregations focused on villages to one consisting of a splintering of populations, many of whom were nomadic, at least on an annual basis."[204]

The reason or reasons for this cultural breakdown are unknown. Climate may have been a contributing factor, or, as some have argued, forests and agricultural soils may have been depleted around individual PPNB sites.[117] Of the settlements that were still occupied, some revealed toolkits marked by aesthetic degeneration. In the semi-desert steppe of Syria, projectile points at the late PPNB settlement of El Kowm (map at fig. 5) were apparently rare and carelessly manufactured, and it appears that some of the finest examples of PPNB weaponry in this region were being crafted by nomadic peoples.[37] Although nomads seldom leave archaeologically detectable traces of their activities, excavators found many stratified layers of campsites without structures (Qdeir PPNB) within this same El Kowm oasis, evidently occupied by nomadic herders of domestic sheep, goats, and cattle. Of the weapons made by these nomadic pastoralists, Cauvin has remarked: "their sophisticated manufacture retains a cohesion with the whole of the previous PPNB."[37]

A sharp decrease in the number and size of settlements in eastern Turkey may indicate a substantial shift to nomadic pastoralism there as well.[169] Nomadic herdsmen had actually been known to this region as early as 7700 BC at the PPNB site of Hayaz (map at fig. 5), which yielded no permanent structures but offered abundant evidence of flint-working and the presence of domestic sheep, goats, and cattle.[191] Farther south, nomadic peoples are believed to have dug pits into the abandoned PPNB site at Tell Ramad near Damascus.[37] Settled village life in this region would not resume until around 6300 BC, by which time the culture of lands to both the east and the west will have been radically transformed.

As we will see in the following chapters, the painted pottery villages that were founded from Iran to Greece between 6500 and 6000 BC represent a profound departure from the traditions of PPNB. Because Greece has enjoyed more archaeological attention than countries that are less receptive to western-sponsored excavations, it offers an excellent starting point for exploring an extraordinary cultural change that affected most of the Middle East as well. Therefore, before investigating contemporary late-seventh-millennium events in Iran and Iraq, we will go first to the Aegean, to set the stage for the arrival of the first farmers of Europe — the small groups of pioneers who brought the grains, animals, and architectural skills that laid the foundation for eight thousand years of Western civilization.

Fig. 10　Characteristics of Early Cultural Periods

Rough reconstruction of events covered in the text from 12,500 to 6000 BC (reading upwards)

CAL BC	Cultural Period	Sub-cultures/Sites mentioned in the text	General Characteristics
6000	*Painted Pottery Neolithic*	Djeitun Halaf Samarra Early Neolithic Greece Hajii Firuz Hassuna Sialk/Cheshmeh Ali	*beginnings of metallurgy* *miniature mortars and pestles* *disappearance of projectile points, bucrania,* 　*skull displays, ceremonial structures* *fine painted pottery* *use of irrigation* *near-total reliance on domestic species* *small "egalitarian" settlement patterns*
Dating of Zarathustra by ancient historians (6500-6200) **6500** *(you are here)*			
7000	*Pre-Pottery Neolithic B*	El Kowm Çatal Höyük 'Ain Ghazal Hayaz Beidha Jericho Abu Hureyra Çayönü Mureybet	*increase of nomadism* *widespread site abandonment* *introduction of pottery* *large "towns" of several thousand* *finely carved pestles* *male statuary associated with the bull* *ornately crafted weaponry* *displays of human skulls* *complex ceremonial structures* *domestic animals as well as plants* *rectangular architecture*
8700			
9500	*Pre-Pottery Neolithic A*	Tell Aswad Jericho Jerf al-Ahmar Mureybet Abu Hureyra	*domestic grain* *further development of projectile points* *separated human skulls* *non-domestic structures* 　*(e.g. Jericho tower and wall)* *hunting and gathering* *mud bricks in round house architecture*
10,000	*Natufian*	Mureybet Abu Hureyra 'Ain Mallaha	*small figurines of raptors, females, bulls* *tanged arrowheads* *sporadic cultivation of wheat and rye* *adornment of the dead* *carved bone sickles* *ground and polished stone artifacts* *microlithic tools* *hunting and gathering* *small clusters of permanent round houses*
12,500			

Late Paleolithic hunter-gatherers

CHAPTER THREE

Early Neolithic Greece, 6400-6000 BC

"The appearance of farming villages in Greece was indeed a profound revolution in human history and brought into existence a way of life that has remained the basis of European society to the present day."

— Curtis Runnels and Priscilla Murray,
Greece Before History

Before 9000 BC the only known inhabitants of Greece were groups of Paleolithic hunters who left flint tools near the fires they laid in mountain and hillside caves. Judging from the animal bones recovered nearby, the smaller flints may have served as the tips of spears or arrows used to hunt wild bison, cattle, and elk. There is little evidence that wild plants served as food, and there are no graves, works of art, or permanent constructions such as walls or hearths. It has been suggested that these cave sites were actually short-term hunting stations, used by groups whose main camps may have been nearer the coast.[195]

If base camps did exist in the coastal regions of Paleolithic Greece, they now lie below the level of the sea. As the glaciers of the last Ice Age melted and retreated, sea levels in the Aegean rose: 150 feet by c. 9000 BC and another 100 feet by 6000 BC.[215] The coastal plains lost to the rising seas are believed to have been the most desirable habitats, with abundant grazing lands threaded by wooded streams and rivers. How quickly the ocean rose is unknown, as is the relationship, if any, of the rising seas to the disappearance of Paleolithic hunters throughout Greece. What we do know is that by the beginning of the tenth millennium, almost all of the Paleolithic caves had been abandoned.

The archaeological record then falls silent, and Greece appears to have remained virtually uninhabited for over a thousand years. At some point in the ninth millennium, perhaps c. 8500 BC, one of the old Paleolithic sites, Franchthi Cave in the Greek Argolid (map at fig. 11), was again occupied.[109] Archaeologists estimate that by this time the rising seas had reduced Franchthi's distance from the coast, perhaps four miles in Paleolithic times, to less than one mile.[195] The identity of the new inhabitants is unknown. They were not yet the Neolithic farmers, and in fact, while PPNB peoples in the Near East were crafting ornate weapons and domesticating wheat and barley, their contemporaries at Franchthi Cave were still using microlithic tools similar to those of the

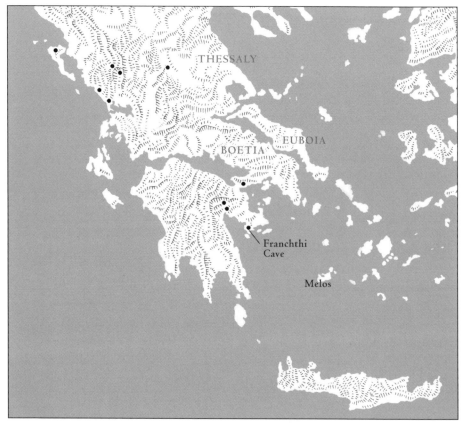

Fig. 11 Mesolithic Greece. Dots represent individual sites. (after Perlès, 2001)

Late Paleolithic (fig. 12) and consuming only wild plants and animals.[173] The presence at Franchthi of obsidian from the island of Melos, some sixty miles across open seas, as well as the remains of deep-sea-dwelling fish, indicate that these people were nevertheless able seafarers. Their boats, believed to have been made of reeds, have not survived.

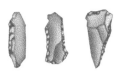

Franchthi Cave is one of a very few known sites — perhaps a dozen — that were occupied during this "Mesolithic" period in Greece (map at fig. 11). Systematic surveys in Euboia and Boetia reveal no detectable human population at this time, and only one site (Theopetra, now under excavation) has been discovered in Thessaly.[173]

Fig. 12 Microlithic tools at Franchthi Cave, ninth millennium. (after Perlès, 2001)

Franchthi Cave would be of singular importance in any case because it is today the only one of the known Greek sites with a published sequence of archaeological deposits showing the transition from foraging to farming.

The First Farmers of Europe

Domesticated plants and animals began to appear at Franchthi Cave during the first half of the seventh millennium, but major cultural changes did not take place until c. 6400 BC, when pottery was introduced into the site.[89] At this time a small village was constructed just outside the mouth of the cave, with rectangular buildings whose mud brick walls were supported by stone foundations. In Thessaly, a handful of settlements also appear to have been founded early in the seventh millennium BC, but there, as at Franchthi Cave, the most dramatic changes on the Thessalian plain took place from c. 6400 to 6000 BC, a time span that defines the Greek "Early Neolithic." As several observers have remarked, the most striking element of Early Neolithic Greece is the sheer number of settlements that were founded at this time.[51] Almost 250 new farming villages are known to have been established during this period, with perhaps 50 more of uncertain date.

Almost as surprising as the number of settlements is the depth of commitment these people had made to the agricultural way of life. Emmer and einkorn wheat, barley, and legumes were cultivated throughout Early

Neolithic Greece, while sheep, goats, cattle, and pigs were kept or herded. Archaeologists have found little evidence of temporary camps, or of villages that did not remain active and occupied for extended periods.[12] Caves were conspicuously avoided during the Early Neolithic period; even at Franchthi the main occupation was in the newly constructed village outside the cave. From the scarcity of wild animals in the faunal remains, the European prehistorian Catherine Perlès has determined that "wild resources were not only under-exploited but deliberately neglected," a finding that she feels testifies to both the importance of, and the symbolic value placed on, domesticated plants and animals by the Early Neolithic settlers of Greece.[173]

As shown in the map at figure 13, the geographical location of Greek sites, along with the appearance of the first known settlers on the island of Crete (at Knossos), suggests that the early farmers came by sea. If so, these Neolithic mariners would have required something more substantial than reed boats to ferry themselves, their domestic animals, and adequate supplies of grain across the Mediterranean. In an analysis of the cargo needed to establish the settlement at Knossos, one team of prehistorians estimated that the founding group was made up of perhaps a dozen families, along with five to ten carefully chosen pairs of each species of animal (cattle, sheep, goats, pigs) to insure viable breeding populations. Adding the grain required for food and seed crops to the human and animal occupants gives a total, by their estimation, of perhaps twenty tons of cargo.[32]

Remains or depictions of boats are again absent, but given the limitations of early Neolithic toolkits, these authors believe that paddled log or hide boats, watertight to prevent the spoiling of seed crops, would have been the most likely forms of craft for the journey. Their hypothesis — that a flotilla of perhaps ten to fifteen vessels, each carrying a ton or two of cargo, transported the founders of Knossos to their new home[32] — may be applied to the settling of Greece as well.

As these researchers further point out, the degree of planning required for each such enterprise would have been extremely high. Embarking from (unknown) ports in the Near East,[173] the boats would most likely have put to sea just after the summer harvest, arriving early enough to locate a suitable site and clear the natural forest before a late-

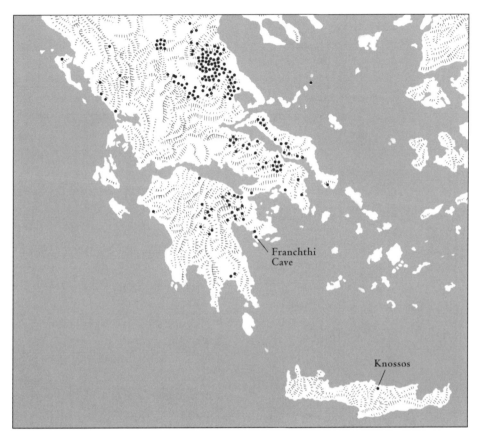

Fig. 13 Early Neolithic Greece, 6400-6000 BC. Dots represent sites or groups of sites. (after Perlès, 2001)

autumn sowing of the initial landfall crop. Because cattle in particular are known to be extremely difficult to feed and water in transit, becoming unmanageable after a few days, watering stops would have been planned at chosen islands in the Cyclades and the time at sea made as brief as possible.[32] Prehistorians still do not know why such a difficult and dangerous migration was undertaken. It was indeed a heroic effort and, in terms of the spread of agriculture, overwhelmingly successful. Five hundred years later, farming would reach the Danube and in five hundred more years, eastern France and Holland,[82] laying, as it spread, the material foundations of European civilization.

A "dazzling burst of innovation"

The Early Neolithic period in Greece is distinguished by what has been called "a fundamental revolution of the economic mode of life and a dazzling burst of innovation in the sphere of material culture."[195] Referring to the "enormous leap" made between c. 6400 and 6000 BC in the art and architecture of Greece, Marija Gimbutas observed that the acceleration of cultural achievement coincided with the appearance of painted pottery, whose motifs she found to be symbolic of renewal and regeneration.[82] As we will see, many of the patterns painted on Greek ceramics appear on the pottery of contemporary sites in the Middle East as well.

Ceramic specialists have pointed out that even the earliest red-and-white painted pottery of Greece, with its small size and limited repertoire of designs, was not technically primitive. These wares are believed to have been made to a standard recipe, requiring a significant investment of time and energy, and their apparent crudeness is attributed to insufficient knowledge and experience rather than any lack of effort on the part of their creators.[221] But since early Greek pots were small, few in number, and of unknown purpose, analysts have questioned why the craft was pursued at all. Pottery could easily have been adopted for household purposes, but nothing indicates the use of these ceramics in cooking, and, given their size and rarity, storage has also been ruled out.

Fig. 14 Motif from ceramic bowl. Sesklo, Thessaly, early sixth millennium BC. (after Theocharis, 1973)

Even with the passage of time and an ongoing improvement in the potters' skill and artistry (fig. 14), these ceramic wares continued to show few signs of use.[173] Motifs did vary from region to region, but, as one authority notes, "adherence to the same basic elements of design (such as geometric patterns) is evidence of some larger unifying principle that we have yet to grasp: one of the mysteries of Neolithic civilization."[195] More than one analyst believes that Early Neolithic Greek ceramics were intentionally kept out of the domestic sphere, reserved for ritual use alone.[173, 221] And yet, with the possible exception of an ambiguous building at Nea Nikomedia, there appear to have been no ceremonial structures within these villages.

Dwellings were generally small and rectangular throughout Early Neolithic Greece, with sun-dried mud bricks used as building materials in some villages and a combination of timber, branches, clay, and mud in others. Excavators found miniature house models which indicate that the clay-covered thatched roofs may have been painted bright colors, with doors and windows decorated by red and white borders.[195] As in the Near East, new dwellings were usually built directly on top of the old ones, creating mounds or "magoulas" that grew higher with each rebuilding of the settlement. The small size of these communities — one to three hundred inhabitants — appears to be a characteristic feature of Early Neolithic Greece.

In contrast to the PPNB culture that dominated the Near East before 6500 BC, arrow and spear heads were virtually unknown in Early Neolithic Greece, although tool-working techniques associated with PPNB were used to prepare obsidian and flint blades for the harvesting of crops. Quite uncertain is the function of the small mushroom-shaped objects (fig. 15a), finely carved and polished, that were found in the earliest Neolithic levels of several Greek sites. (For example, those at Achilleion, a typical site of the Sesklo culture in southern Thessaly, appeared only in the earliest phase, c. 6400 BC.[83]) Although they are sometimes referred to as "earstuds" by archaeologists in Greece — and as "labrets" by excavators who have uncovered their counterparts in contemporary Middle Eastern sites — there is actually no certain evidence that these elements were worn on the body. Another prehistorian has recently suggested that they might instead have been used to hold together woven or leather clothing.[173]

In Greece and elsewhere, these "studs" appear concurrently with engraved "stamp seals," whose use is equally mysterious (fig. 15b). As their motifs fall within a small range of geometric patterns that are known as far east as the Indus valley, an earlier theory that the seals might have been used as individual identification markers has been questioned, and a more recent interpretation suggests their use as textile stamps.[173] Polished stone axes, mounted in antler sockets set into wooden handles, were effective woodworking tools, as they had been in PPNB sites, while miniature versions, "small jewel-like axes meticulously sculpted in green stone," were apparently of symbolic value (fig. 15c).[83]

Although the remains of textiles have not survived, the presence of spindle whorls in these settlements suggests that the weaver's craft was now practiced in Greece, as it had been earlier in the Near East. The designs used by Neolithic Greek weavers may have been similar to those found on the pottery, which included dark and light triangles or diamonds, checkerboards, and chevrons (fig. 16). Today, houses throughout the east Mediterranean world are filled with woven textiles or *kilims*, and one suspects it may always have been so. In fact, prehistorians have noted the astonishing endurance of the fundamental way of life that began with these small farming communities. Grounded in agriculture and animal husbandry, Early Neolithic Greek farmers lived in a way that was not unlike rural life in the Balkans into the eighteenth or nineteenth centuries AD.[195]

The same may be said of Iran and Iraq, where life in many rural areas has changed little since the seventh millennium BC. In the next chapter we will find that the new farmers of the Middle East shared a great many elements with their contemporaries in Greece—similar settlement patterns (small rectangular houses in villages of fewer than three hundred people), domestic crops and animals (hexaploid wheat, barley, legumes,

Fig. 15a Neolithic Greek "studs," Achilleion,
　　　seventh millennium BC (after Gimbutas, 1989)
Fig. 15b Clay stamp seal from Nea Nikomedia (after Rodden 1965)
Fig. 15c Miniature greenstone axe (after Gimbutas, 1989)

Fig. 16 Geometric designs, Early Neolithic Greek pottery (after Otto, 1985)

flax; sheep, goats, cattle, pigs), carefully carved studs and stamp seals, and fine geometrically painted pottery that appears to have been used for neither cooking nor storage. Recognizable ceremonial structures were virtually absent in both Greece and the Middle East at this time, as were the elaborate weapons and other "symbols of virility"[37] that had characterized the PPNB culture of the preceding period. A further resemblance: the lack of a satisfactory explanation for the immense and enduring cultural changes that took place in both regions in the last half of the seventh millennium.

Colonists, Native Peoples, or Both?

Recent excavations in Greece have stimulated a great deal of thought with regard to questions of who these new settlers were and why farming was so widely adopted at this time. As we saw in the last chapter, an agricultural economy had been known to the Near East since the ninth millennium, and sedentary communities were present as early as the twelfth. Why did permanent settlements only now appear in Greece, and why were these settlers so intent on cultivating the land? The effort to answer those questions has been described as follows by one team of prehistorians:

> "Despite many years of investigation of the subject,…the transition from mainly hunter-gatherer Mesolithic societies to predominantly farming Neolithic ones remains a major unresolved problem in European prehistory, with the reasons for the transition and the manner, the rate, and the mechanism of this transformation all being subjects of debate and controversy."[246]

In attempting to understand why the agricultural way of life spread to Europe, archaeologists have focused primarily on the question of who the new farmers were — immigrants or native peoples. Clearly some of them were newcomers: certain tool working techniques, polished greenstone axes, and stone grinding implements were all known in the Near East before making their first appearance in the new agricultural settlements of Greece. And in spite of the difficulties that would have been involved in transporting people, plants, and animals across the Mediterranean Sea, the domestic species found in these European sites are all known to have been cultivated or kept in Near Eastern settlements for a millennium or more.

The wild forms of most of these plants and animals were not native to Europe, and no transitional forms have been recovered that would indicate local domestication.[246] Furthermore, in contrast to the great variety of wild plants consumed by the pre-Neolithic residents of Greece (the Mesolithic menu at Franchthi Cave included wild olives, bulbs, roots, nuts, legumes, and leafy plants), the economy of Neolithic Greece was based almost entirely on domesticated species. What one pair of analysts found striking about the use of wild plants and animals in Early Neolithic Greece was how little there was of it.[51]

But scholars find evidence of continuity with earlier hunter-gatherer traditions as well, demonstrated, for example, in the style and range of stone tools at Franchthi.[109] It has also been argued that newcomers to Greece would have been unable to effectively explore an unknown landscape without at least some help from the existing inhabitants.[235] And while it is true that certain ceramic patterns, as well as the non-culinary nature of early Greek pottery, suggests a kinship with the fine painted pottery spreading across the Middle and Near East at this time, the evolution of Greek ceramic motifs has been judged specifically European. The fact that each region quickly developed a different variation on a general style[51] is seen as an indication of existing native traditions that were then transferred to the newly acquired craft of painted pottery.[13]

Preliminary mitochondrial DNA evidence now suggests that all of these observations may actually be correct, and that both immigrants and native peoples were involved in the settling of Greece. The geographic distribution of mtDNA lineages indicates a rapid penetration into southeast Europe by small groups of Near Eastern agriculturists, followed by a gradual intermixing with more numerous indigenous inhabitants.[187, 181] This new information supports the opinion, now generally held, that the spread of agriculture into southeastern Europe was accomplished by migrating farmers in combination with what one prehistorian called "the conversion of local populations."[82]

But if these findings tell us more about who the new farmers were — both colonists *and* indigenes — they compound the question of motive. We must now ask not only why peoples from the Near East would have risked the dangerous voyage to Greece (as noted above, there is at present no evidence to sustain an earlier-held assumption that rising population densities caused surplus farmers to "spill over" into Europe[68]), but also why indigenous hunter-gatherers would so readily have given up their traditional way of life. There is no indication of a shortage of wild resources in Europe, and in fact the evidence at Franchthi Cave suggests that Greece was particularly rich in wild foods at this time.[173]

As mentioned in the opening chapter, Jacques Cauvin has written persuasively of the importance of ideology and religious belief in the *page 6* great collective movements of history — and presumably of prehistory as well. He has specifically argued that "the amazingly positive welcome" which the new arrivals in Greece received from native populations can only be understood in terms of ideology. In his view, the colonists themselves are likely to have been joined in their movement across the land by newly converted indigenous peoples, much like the North African Berbers who, having themselves adopted Islam, then assisted the Arabs in spreading the Muslim faith through Spain. Cauvin's conclusion: "Nothing prevents us from envisaging analogous phenomena in the Neolithic, since so many other explanations fall short. Such an explanation would also help us to understand why a new religion might everywhere have accompanied the new economy, the one being the secret of the other."[37]

Could that new religion have been based on the teachings of Zarathustra? In the following chapter we will find that Cauvin's reasoning may hold true for Neolithic Iran and Iraq as well as Europe. The multitude of new Middle Eastern farming settlements established after c. 6500 BC, almost all of which were founded on virgin soil, bore unmistakable similarities to their contemporaries in Greece. And although archaeological information will be more limited, particularly with regard to Iran, we will find that some of these Middle Eastern settlers seem to have been more advanced technologically than their Greek counterparts —which could mean that the impulse that sent farmers into Europe in the last half of the seventh millennium actually originated in Iraq or Iran.

CHAPTER FOUR

Painted Pottery Cultures of the Middle East, 6500-6000 BC

"The transition from aceramic to ceramic cultures remains one of the most intriguing problems of Near Eastern prehistory. After the long development and diffusion of farming and the remarkable flourishing of the PPNB cultures, nearly all the sites were abandoned and the general territorial occupation changed. Few sites continued to be occupied into the following period, and even fewer uninterruptedly, while the early pottery traditions were established in new sites, very often in previously unoccupied areas."

– Isabella Caneva,
"Early Farmers on the Cilician Coast"

The archaeology of the Middle East suggests a date of c. 6500 BC for the dawn of a cultural reformation that rejected the cult excesses of the preceding PPNB period while renewing the commitment to an agricultural way of life. Destined to range far wider than PPNB, this final critical phase of the Neolithic Revolution was to exert an immensely more powerful influence on the course of human history. As in Greece, those responsible for this "explosive expansion"[244] of agricultural settlements were potters as well as farmers, and they painted their fine ceramics with dark-light checkerboard motifs as well as crosses, circles, and whirl patterns.

As agriculture and rectangular architecture were no longer new to the Middle East at this time, perhaps the most remarkable aspect of the painted pottery communities that spread across Iran and Iraq is the "conspicuous absence" of arrow and spear heads.[170] Considering the proximity of some of these new sites to settlements of the preceding period, the break with the PPNB weapons tradition is even more striking here than in Greece. Seldom in these early Middle Eastern farming communities is there more than an occasional appearance of the armaments associated with PPNB, and then only in base levels. Accordingly, the favored diagnostic tool for Neolithic archaeologists now shifts from arrow and spear heads to painted pottery, the fine ceramics that are the hallmark of this new era.

page 23

We will begin our investigation in northern Iraq, where the earliest of the painted pottery styles is associated with the "Hassuna" culture of the upper Tigris region. The eponymous site (map at fig. 17) was founded c. 6500 BC, with projectile points similar to those associated with PPNB present only in the lowest level. Continuing the tradition of a soft, chaff-tempered "archaic" ware that was already known to the region, Hassuna-style painted pottery originally featured simple geometric designs in red on a cream-colored background.[148] But the color of the motifs soon changed from a uniform red to a spectrum ranging from dark reddish brown to almost black, believed to be the darkening effects of higher firing temperatures on iron-oxide-based pigments. Local designs continued, but several new elements appeared at this time, among them the use of pattern on the inside of bowls.[128]

Hassuna-style pottery was present as well in the earliest settlement at Nineveh (map at fig. 17), indicating to archaeologists that this very famous old site was also founded in the middle of the seventh millennium.[149] Similar pottery has been discovered in the base levels of several other newly founded agricultural settlements in the upper Tigris region, but the radiocarbon readings of all of the Hassuna sites are apparently too close for analysts to determine exactly where this new cultural expression began.

To the northeast, pottery designs similar to those on Hassuna ceramics appeared in sites of the "Hajii Firuz" culture of northwestern Iran, which included perhaps a dozen new agricultural communities in the area around Lake Urmia.[222] Again dating to the mid-seventh millennium BC, the excavated villages of Hajii Firuz and Yanik Tepe (map at fig. 17) were composed of small rectangular mud-brick houses with raised hearths and occasional traces of red-stained or -plastered floors.[34] None of these farming villages was over one or two acres in size, and excavators found few

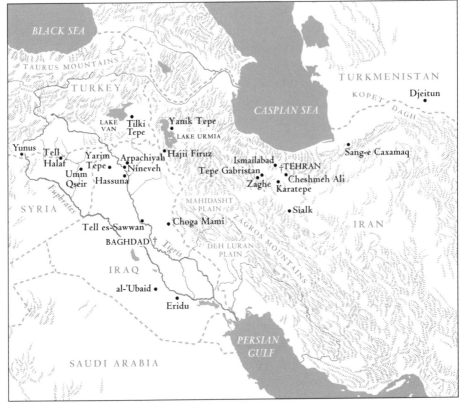

Fig. 17 Painted pottery sites mentioned in the text, 6500 – 5500 BC. † = *modern cities*

signs of social stratification. Earlier settlements are unknown in this region, and the origin of the Hajii Firuz culture is again a mystery. Archaeologists have noted, however, that this Lake Urmia pottery reveals signs of contact with the Iranian plateau as well as with the Hassuna culture of Iraq.[222]

Moving southward, similarities to the pottery of both the Hassuna and Hajii Firuz cultures have been identified in the ceramics of thirteen known agricultural settlements founded at this time in the Mahidasht plain of the central Zagros mountains of western Iran. Still farther south, the pattern of greatly increased settlement activity is repeated in the Deh Luran plain of southwestern Iran, an area between the lower Tigris and the Zagros foothills that was only sparsely settled in the previous period.[102] Here as elsewhere archaeologists have been unable to identify a mechanism such as trade or transhumance (the seasonal movement of herds) that could account for the stylistic and cultural similarities that clearly obtain between different regions in this period.

Hassuna-style pottery may also have been present in the lowest levels of the newly founded settlement at Tell es-Sawwan (map at fig. 17). If so, it was soon joined by an even more richly decorated, chocolate-brown-on-buff pottery known as "Samarra" ware (so named because ceramics of this style were first discovered in a prehistoric cemetery beneath the medieval city of Samarra, which lies just north of Tell es-Sawwan). The rudimentary motifs which had appeared on Hassuna wares seem to have been incorporated into new and more complex patterns on Samarran pottery (fig. 18). These new ceramics then enjoyed a wide distribution to the north, appearing in strata above Hassuna wares at both Nineveh and the site of Hassuna itself by approximately 6300 BC.[149]

Although prehistorians originally believed that the Samarran culture came from Iran,[31] it now seems more likely that these were indigenous peoples of the middle Tigris valley who chose to settle in the relatively low-lying territory between the rain-fed farming land of northern Iraq and the arid delta of the south. Peculiarities of form in certain cultivars (hexaploid bread wheat, six-row barley, large-seed flax) at Tell es-Sawwan

Fig. 18 Samarran ceramics from (a) Tell es-Sawwan and (b) the site of Hassuna, late seventh millennium BC (after Braidwood et al, 1944; Lloyd and Sefar, 1945)

a   b

Fig. 19 Cruciform patterns on (a) the pottery of Eridu in southern Iraq and (b) Samarran ceramics (after Mellaart, 1975; Braidwood et al, 1944)

indicate that irrigation was now being practiced.[148] The first recorded traces of irrigating canals were in fact found at the Samarran site of Choga Mami (map at fig. 17) northeast of present-day Baghdad, where evidence of domestic cattle suggested to some observers that these farmers may have already been using cattle to plow their fields.[68, 164]

Samarran potters took full advantage of the inner surfaces of their open bowls to create patterns based on the circle, the cross, and prominently, the principle of motion. Not only the "whirl patterns" on shallow bowls (fig. 18b) but also the taller vessels, with their horizontal bands of flowing designs (fig. 18a), create an impression of movement. Occasional motifs of animals, plants, and even stylized human forms also appeared on Samarran wares, but it is the quality of the geometric designs in particular that led one observer to conclude that "the people who modelled and painted such vessels were undoubtedly great artists."[194]

Patterns associated with Samarran pottery have also been found on the ceramics of Eridu (map at fig. 17), the earliest recorded settlement in the land later to be known as Sumer. How the first farming communities of the lower Euphrates might have acquired the skills necessary for survival in such an arid environment is unknown, but excavators have found a system of small canals, up to three miles long, that apparently served to irrigate their fields.[68] The lowest level at Eridu, estimated to c. 6300 BC, yielded mud-brick architecture and fine painted pottery whose chocolate-colored cruciform patterns are particularly reminiscent of Samarran designs (fig. 19).

But in spite of their many similarities, the differences between these mid-to-late seventh millennium cultures left one authority with "the distinct impression that each area displays an essentially local though not an isolated development."[165] Joan Oates believes that a number of different ethnic groups were probably represented among these new settlers, some of whom may earlier have been mobile hunters or food gatherers whose traces are less susceptible to archaeological detection. Why these various peoples now chose a settled way of life, and where they got the architectural and agricultural know-how, are unanswered questions.

The Iranian Plateau and the Northeast

Archaeological information from the Iranian plateau is more limited, but the earliest settlements at Sialk and Cheshmeh Ali (map at fig. 17) are known to have contained pottery similar to that of the Hassuna phase in Iraq.[63] The investigation of both of these Iranian sites took place in the 1930s and thus lacked today's refined technologies for the recovery and analysis of plant remains.[79, 197] Nevertheless, the presence at Sialk of at least two domesticates (barley and goat) vouch for its standing as an agricultural community. Miniature mortars and pestles were also recovered at Sialk, fashioned in clay as well as stone. Early ceramics included sherds similar to the red-on-cream "archaic" painted ware found elsewhere at the end of the preceding period, but here, as in the early Hassuna pottery, simple patterns were already beginning to be painted on the inner surfaces of open bowls.[63] The "double-axe" symbol at the center of a Sialk bowl (fig. 20) would become a familiar element among the pottery designs of both Iran and Iraq in this period.

As with the painted pottery communities of Iraq, the origin of the Sialk culture of Iran (which includes the early phase of occupation at the site of Cheshmeh Ali) is unknown. Similar pottery was found at Zaghe[158] (map at fig. 17), where geometrically painted wares have been compared to those of

Fig. 20   Ceramic vessel from Sialk I, central Iran c. 6500 – 6000 BC (after Ghirschman, 1938)

the Hajii Firuz sites in northwest Iran as well as to the ceramics of Sialk and Cheshmeh Ali. According to one pair of analysts, more distant ties to all of these Iranian sites can be found in the Hassuna and Samarra painted pottery cultures of Iraq.[226] In fact, if the turquoise made into beads at the Samarran site of Tell es-Sawwan originated in northeast Iran, as archaeologists surmise,[147] the route by which it reached the Iraqi lowlands may well have passed through the area now occupied by the Sialk culture. But again, the direction of cultural influence—east to west or west to east—is unclear.

In northeastern Iran itself, archaeologists have discovered several mounds at Sang-e Caxamaq in the fertile Gurgan plain (map at fig. 17). Only two of these tells have been investigated, but the results chronicle a significant change in this region in the last half of the seventh millennium. The older settlement, which yielded the red-plastered floors associated with *page 22* the PPNB period, had apparently been abandoned before the advent of painted pottery. In contrast, the later mound at Sang-e Caxamaq contained geometrically painted ceramics and several other elements, including miniature mortars and pestles, that were absent from the older tell.[137, 196]

Sang-e Caxamaq is believed to be related to a chain of farming communities that sprang up along the edge of the Kopet Dagh of Turkmenistan late in the seventh millennium.[94] Small, compact villages of mud-brick rectangular houses and domestic animals and crops were again characteristic of this "Djeitun" culture, which may have achieved irrigation by damming up small rivulets of nearby mountain streams.[147] Although early Djeitun pottery was primarily a simple red-on-buff ware, "distinguished by its conservatism,"[196] some of the painted pottery motifs—as well as the miniature mortars and pestles at the site of Djeitun itself (map at fig. 17)—show connections to the Iranian plateau.

In trying to reconstruct the founding of the Djeitun settlements, one archaeologist finds it likely that a relatively small population of farmers and stockbreeders from outside the region "dispersed among the communities of hunters, fishers and food collectors, introducing agricultural practices, architectural traditions, and ceramics."[58] If this is true—and it seems a logical reconstruction of the way many if not all of these new Middle Eastern painted pottery settlements were founded—we must ask, as we did in discussing the Greek Neolithic, who were these *page 37* newcomers, and why were they interested in converting local populations to an agricultural way of life? And again, why would the indigenous hunter-gatherers of Turkmenistan and elsewhere in the Middle East have so readily given up their traditional way of life?

Cheshmeh Ali

Back on the Iranian plateau, an extraordinarily fine type of painted pottery known as the "Cheshmeh Ali" style was evolving out of the original Sialk style ceramics. As noted above, the site of Cheshmeh Ali itself lies on the northern plateau (map at fig. 17), near present-day Tehran and some 120 miles north of the settlement at Sialk. Unfortunately, our main source of information about this site comes from a sounding made in the 1930s, and even these findings remain largely unpublished.[197, 138] Still less is known of other northern plateau sites belonging to the Cheshmeh Ali culture (e.g., Karatepe and Ismailabad), but the presence of Sialk-style pottery in the base levels of the site of Cheshmeh Ali indicates that this settlement, like Sialk, was founded midway in the seventh millennium. Neither of these villages is believed to have contained more than two hundred people.[138]

Cheshmeh Ali style pottery would eventually spread into virtually all parts of Iran. Painted in black or dark brown on a pale orange-to-red surface, ceramic vessels of this period include "eggshell thin" cups, fired so hard that they produce a "clink" when struck.[226] The alternation of dark and light cones (or sets of double-axes) formed, in one known case,

Fig. 21
Cheshmeh Ali style
bowls and sherds,
sixth millennium BC
(after Ghirschman,
1938; Maleki, 1968)

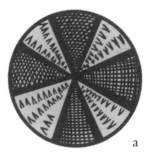
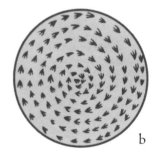

a

b

a pair of Maltese-like crosses accompanied by indications of movement (fig. 21a). Other Cheshmeh Ali design elements include spirals (fig. 21b), whirl patterns (fig. 21c), cruciform or "wheeled cross" designs (fig. 21d), checkerboards and "fringed swastikas" (fig. 21e). The majority of designs are geometric, although the ancient Iranian tradition of stylized plants and animals (primarily the mountain goat) also had its beginnings in the ceramics of this period.[138] The presence of Cheshmeh Ali style pottery in the upper levels of the settlement at Zaghe to the west, Sang-e Caxamaq to the northeast, and sites in southwestern Iran (the Surkh and Choga Mami Transitional phases)[226] verifies the pan-Iranian universality of a tradition that originated in the middle of the seventh millennium BC.

Shared Themes

In spite of the uneven archaeological information, the main themes of this period are clearly defined and may briefly be summarized as follows. From Turkmenistan and the Iranian plateau to the Iraqi lowlands and westward to Greece, free-standing rectangular architecture, painted pottery, and domestic crops and animals were not the only elements held in common —partially or wholly—by the new settlements. Almost all were founded on virgin soil, and, in contrast to earlier PPNB communities of several thousand inhabitants, few seem to have contained more than perhaps two or three hundred people. Human skulls, bulls' horns, and male statuary were gone, and with the exception of what may have been a burial shrine or sanctuary at the base level of Tell-es-Sawwan, ceremonial structures

c

d

e

were also missing. The arrow and spear heads that had dominated the toolkits of the preceding PPNB culture were occasionally present in base levels of these new sites, but in each case they then vanished, leaving a preponderance of "agricultural" blades.[118] Studs and stamp seals were broadly diffused, while miniature mortars and pestles seem to have been largely confined to Iran.

Cultural differences among the new settlements of this period suggest that their inhabitants were primarily local peoples, perhaps of different ethnicities, whose former (presumably mobile) way of life left no traces in the archaeological record. And though levels of sophistication in ceramic technique varied from region to region, the painted patterns themselves reveal similar elements of design, suggesting a shared symbolic tradition. Nowhere do we find evidence that the fine painted pottery was used for cooking, suggesting, as noted earlier in Greece, a ritual purpose that may have been associated with these shared beliefs. Finally, archaeologists admit that they do not know the nature of the connections between the many different regions whose painted ceramics show contact with one another. Nor do they know why, in the last half of the seventh millennium BC, so many people, living in such diverse ecosystems, would suddenly have chosen to settle and cultivate the land.

Halaf

One final, particularly intriguing, painted pottery tradition remains to be considered. Running parallel with the further development of Sialk/ Cheshmeh Ali ceramics on the Iranian plateau, the pottery of the "Halaf" culture first began to surface late in the seventh millennium in northern Iraq. Here Halafian ceramics followed upon, and slightly overlapped, Samarran pottery at both Hassuna and Nineveh.[128] (The eponymous site, Tell Halaf [map at fig. 17], overlooks the Khabur river near today's Turkish-Syrian border.)

The ceramics of Halaf are often described as the finest prehistoric pottery in Iraq.[239] Fashioned from selected clays, tempered with fine sand to produce a paste of uniform consistency, Halafian vessels often gave the impression of great delicacy.[154] Thin-walled and hard-fired, these ceramics, like those of Cheshmeh Ali, "clink" when struck. Formed in an extensive variety of shapes, Halafian pottery was usually painted in lustrous black or red-brown on an apricot- or cream-colored slip. And again like the Iranian (and Samarran) potters, the Halafians occasionally portrayed the figures of animals, here most frequently the stylized heads of bulls (e.g., fig. 22a), in addition to their work with purely geometric designs, again featuring cruciform or "wheeled cross" patterns (fig. 22, b and c).

Advances in kiln construction and the use of highly ferruginous clays allowed Halaf potters to fire their wares at extremely high temperatures, which appear to have been painstakingly controlled for the purpose of obtaining the desired colors and accentuating themes of light and darkness. As one analyst remarked, "the Halafians worked for contrast,"[85] and indeed, checkered patterns were among their favorites (fig. 23). Pairs of dark and light triangles inside other squares often formed fields of positive and negative images of the double-axe.

As shown in the Halafian vessel at figure 2, checkered designs were often used as a border or frame for interior polychrome centerpieces that have yet to be surpassed in the ceramic arts. Indeed, in spite of the noted homogeneity of style, the wares of Halaf were largely individual works of art, with no one piece the exact replica of another.[136] And again, although the patterns on these ceramics seem very likely to have been symbolic in nature, ceremonial structures were absent from these sites.

Halafian settlements did contain several types of "studs," which are more

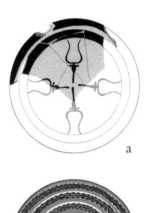

a

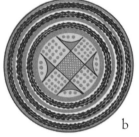

b

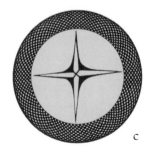

c

Fig. 22 Hand-built open bowls from the sixth-millennium Halafian site of Arpachiyah, northern Iraq (after Mallowan and Rose, 1935)

Fig. 23 Geometric patterns common to Halafian painted pottery (after Mallowan and Rose, 1935)

often called "labrets" by excavators in Iraq (fig. 24) and interpreted as lip or ear ornaments.[4] Amulets and seals from the Halafian site of Arpachiyah were carved in patterns similar to those painted on the pottery, including the wheeled-cross and double-axe motifs that were ubiquitous at this time (fig. 25). The occasional presence of arrowheads and human skulls in Halaf sites, as well as the bull imagery on ceramics and amulets, suggests a connection to the PPNB culture of the preceding period, but Halafian structures ("tholoi") were based on round as well as rectangular forms (fig. 26). The round-house tradition is usually associated with nomadic peoples, and it has been suggested that the Halafians may formerly have been nomadic herdsmen who had newly taken up settled farming.[147]

By the middle of the sixth millennium, Halafian settlements extended from the hills east of the Tigris to Lake Van in the north (Tilki Tepe, map at fig. 17) and west to the western bend of the Syrian Euphrates, creating what has been termed "one of the most homogenous prehistoric cultures anywhere in the world."[124] The influence of Halaf was even more widely spread than the culture itself. In well-surveyed areas like the Mahidasht Plain of western Iran, excavators have counted over sixty sites in the eastern Halafian tradition known as "J-ware."[102] To the west, the influence of this dynamic culture has been detected in sites on the Mediterranean coast and even, in the opinion of some analysts, in central and southern Greece.[233] According to one observer, the impact of Halaf was largely the work of individuals who "peacefully invaded a wide area and mingled with the local population."[194] Why the Halafians sought to spread their influence, and why they seem to have been accepted in almost all regions, are questions for which satisfactory answers have yet to emerge.

Fig. 24 Carved stone "labrets" from Tell Sabi Abyad (after Akkermans, 1993)

In the fifth millennium Halaf was displaced by the 'Ubaid culture of southern Iraq, named after the small mound of al-'Ubaid (map at fig. 17) near what would later become the famed Sumerian city of Ur. Believed to have been an indigenous development following upon the introduction of agriculture into the southern delta, the 'Ubaid culture is marked both by pottery inferior to that of Halaf and by the advent of temple architecture, anticipating the beginning of Sumerian civilization and the early Mesopotamian city-states.[157] The relatively few 'Ubaid vessels that bear painted designs are rather crudely fashioned, and one suspects that the values of the Halafian potters may not have been shared by the peoples of southern Iraq. In any case, connections between Iraq and the Iranian plateau appear to have weakened at this time.

In a later chapter we will find that the painted pottery tradition as a whole came to an end earlier in the west than in eastern Iran, where the painting of ceramic wares was still practiced in the third millennium BC.[213] We will also explore the possibility that an ideology which was expressed in the ceramic designs was then conserved in the oral tradition of Iran.

An example of such enduring conservatism is clearly documented in the agricultural way of life that was established alongside the painted pottery traditions in late seventh millennium Iran. Prehistorians agree that the fundamental pattern of farming and animal husbandry that characterized the countryside of Iran into modern times was formed in the period that concerns us here. And in this sense, as one points out, "the period provides the foundation on which all later Iranian civilizations were built."[102]

Fig. 25 Halaf miniatures (wheeled cross, bull's head, sickle, double-axe) from Arpachiyah, Iraq, sixth millennium BC (after Mallowan and Rose, 1935)

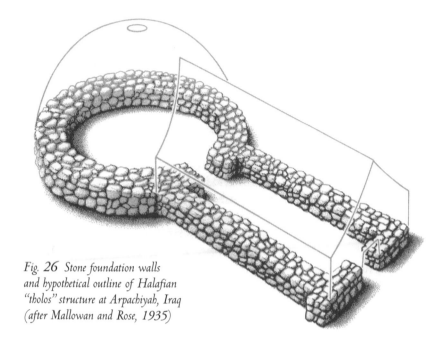

*Fig. 26 Stone foundation walls
and hypothetical outline of Halafian
"tholos" structure at Arpachiyah, Iraq
(after Mallowan and Rose, 1935)*

Did this period also provide the *religious* foundation for the greatest of all later Iranian civilizations? For the Greek and Roman historians of antiquity, there was only one Persian religion, founded by the Iranian prophet whom several of those ancient scholars placed in the last half of the seventh millennium. The credibility of their claims will be explored in the next chapter, along with what is known of Zarathustra's life and teachings. We will then be in a better position to compare his vision with the profound changes we have just observed in lands from Turkmenistan to Greece after 6500 BC.

CHAPTER FIVE

Zarathustra's Life and Teachings

"He who cultivates grain cultivates righteousness,
and promotes and nurtures... the religion
with a hundred new dwelling places."

— *Zend-Avesta, Vendidad* III.3.31

Among the founders of the world's great religions, Zarathustra is undoubtedly the most obscure, at least to modern readers. For many people today, his name is familiar only through Friedrich Nietzsche's *Thus Spake Zarathustra*, a nineteenth-century literary classic in which the teachings of the prophet were manipulated to fit Nietzsche's own philosophical message.[160] But in the Greco-Roman world of antiquity, Zarathustra (Greek Zoroaster) was regarded as a figure of immense stature, not only the founder of Persian religion but "the precursor and voucher of antiquity's own wisdom, both pagan and Christian."[59] In the modern era, the many conflicting legends surrounding the prophet originally led skeptics to doubt his historical existence altogether, but scholars today agree that Zarathustra was indeed a living figure — if an extremely elusive one.

There is considerably less agreement about when he lived. The *Zend-Avesta*, the body of surviving texts that form the ancient canon of the Zoroastrian tradition, does not place the prophet in time. Zoroastrian writings of the ninth century AD put forth 618, 628, or 630 BC as the time of his birth, but those dates are considered impossibly young by many twentieth-century Western analysts. Citing linguistic considerations, these scholars have offered the second millennium, c. 1500-1200 BC, as a more likely time frame for Zarathustra.[28, 45] A third set of dates, recorded by several well-respected Greek and Roman historians of antiquity, places the prophet in the last half of the seventh millennium, between c. 6500 and 6200 BC. These ancient claims have largely been ignored by modern scholarship and are in fact unknown to most archaeologists. But the extraordinary, and as yet unexplained, cultural transformations in the last half of the seventh millennium — the focus of the preceding two chapters — prompt a closer look at the literature of antiquity.

The seventh millennium dating of Zarathustra was articulated not only by several different individuals living in different centuries, but also in several distinct phrasings, an indication that these ancient historians were not just perpetuating a well-known "mythic" convention. For example, in the fifth century BC Xanthus is said to have written in his *Lydian History* that Zoroaster lived six thousand years before the Persian King Xerxes crossed the Hellespont in his assault on the Greeks (c. 480 BC), giving us a date of c. 6480 BC.[57] A century later Eudoxus of Cnidus placed Zoroaster six thousand years before the death of Plato, or c. 6350 BC, a view that Pliny claimed was shared by Aristotle.[177] And in the second century AD, the Roman historian Plutarch wrote that "Zoroaster the Magian lived, so they record, five thousand years before the Siege of Troy" (c. 1200 BC), or c. 6200 BC.[178] This latter estimation is believed to have originated with Hermodorus the Platonist,[57] who was also known for his calculations of the date of Zoroaster.[49]

Without investigating the archaeological evidence for or against these ancient claims, modern Zoroastrian scholars have chosen to defend one or the other of the more recent chronologies mentioned above, either c. 1500-1200 BC or c. 630 BC. Each of these positions has been shown to be vulnerable to criticism from the opposing quarter, however, and the scholarly dispute over the dating of the prophet appears to reflect a larger and more general conflict within the field of Zoroastrian studies. As one observer remarked, the discipline itself has long been "an academic battlefield divided in radically opposed views with no conciliation in sight."[49]

Part of the problem lies in the lack of archaeological evidence supporting either of those more recent placements of Zarathustra in time.[122] By itself this absence of archaeological support would not necessarily invalidate those chronologies, for the very nature of the

Zoroastrian religion works against a historical study based on sacred monuments or temples. As Cicero pointed out in the first century BC, the Persians believed it wrong to confine their deities to temples, "for the entire world is the temple of the gods."[44] Even during the period when Zoroastrianism was the official religion of the Persian empire (550-330 BC), the scarcity of sacred architecture leaves present-day religious historians almost entirely dependent on textual materials.[49]

Unfortunately, the texts are only slightly more helpful. Perhaps three-fourths of the original *Zend-Avesta* is believed to be lost, and what remains is, in the words of one authority, "an assorted mixture whose layers are so numerous and intertwined that it is difficult if not impossible to discern its structure and trace its history."[111] What does remain of the Avesta consists of three primary types of scripture: (1) the *Gathas*, a collection of hymns attributed to Zarathustra himself and often addressed directly to the supreme deity he called Ahura Mazda, the "Wise Lord"; (2) a group of *Yashts*, songs in praise of archaic divinities usually associated with one or another aspect of nature; and (3) the *Vendidad*, which is largely devoted to religious and moral precepts and purifications. Beyond the Avesta, the greater Zoroastrian tradition encompasses a myriad of later accounts from Persian and Islamic sources that may or may not have value as history.

The Avesta itself was not written down until the Sasanian period (224-651 AD), before which time these texts had been handed on orally by generations of Iranian priests. Scholars recognize that one of the difficulties presented by oral traditions is that the stage at which a text is finally preserved often tells us little about when it was composed or how it might have evolved down to that point.[28] With respect to the Avesta, one authority observes: "How much of its contents dates from the earliest period, and how much of it was rewritten to make the past agree with the realities and beliefs of the time in which it was composed is, of course, open to question."[161]

Interpreting the *Gathas*

Zarathustra's own hymns, the *Gathas*, are particularly difficult to translate, with hardly a verse finding an unchallenged interpretation. Although he is considered to be the first person within the Indo-European family of languages who speaks to us as an individual and whose message we can comprehend,* less than half of the Gathic material is actually understood today.[111] The archaic Iranian language presents tremendous difficulties to the interpreter of these obscure hymns, a problem that one observer believes is best illustrated by comparing several translations of the *Gathas*, each made by a competent scholar — and each strikingly different from the others.[161] The disparities in these translations may be due in part to the likelihood, expressed by another authority, that the way in which each translator interprets the *Gathas* depends on where he places Zarathustra in time,[45] a possibility that led me to use several different translations in working with these hymns.

Scholars do agree that the *Gathas* are considerably more ancient than the *Yashts* and the *Vendidad*, which together comprise the so-called "Younger Avesta." Not only do the Gathic hymns appear to be a good deal older linguistically than even the oldest parts of the Younger Avesta,[26] but the same characters who speak and act with immediacy in the *Gathas* are represented in the Younger Avesta as belonging to the remote past. As one interpreter remarked, to go from the *Gathas* to the Younger Avesta is to go "from the land of reality to the land of fable... [We leave] in the one a toiling prophet, to meet in the other a fantastic demi-god."[152] But even the Younger Avesta is believed to be immensely old, and many scholars believe that it contains a great deal of material that faithfully reflects the original teachings of Zarathustra.[46]

The close ties between Iranians and Indians, once apparently a single "Indo-Iranian" branch of the greater Indo-European family, have caused some interpreters to look instead, or as well, to the linguistically related *Rigveda* of India for help in translating the Gathic hymns. The numerous isoglosses shared by Indic and Iranian languages include the common use of the word "airya" (Old Persian) or "arya" (Old Indic) when speaking of themselves. (The name of the country "Iran" is derived from this root, as is the now-contaminated term, "Aryan.")[205] But one prominent

---

Indo-European languages include those of Europe (with the exception of Finnish, Basque, and Hungarian) as well as the languages historically associated with Iran and India.

Zoroastrian scholar points out that while the *Rigveda* may be an excellent source of information concerning an archaic Indo-Iranian religion, it is useless for analyzing the content of the *Gathas*, for Zarathustra's hymns seem to express a "radical change in religious ideas that looks like a revolution with respect to the Indo-Iranian religion, whose most faithful image is considered to be the *Rigveda*."[111] Therefore, if the surviving *Gathas* represent only a fragment of the teachings of Zarathustra — and a partially understood fragment at that — the Younger Avesta is likely to be a more reliable source than the *Rigveda* for interpreting these hymns and reconstructing the prophet's original vision.

The value of the Younger Avestan material is clearly demonstrated with regard to the place of agriculture in that vision. References to farming in the existing *Gathas* are ambiguous and open to more than one interpretation, but in the Younger Avesta the importance of the agricultural way of life is made so explicit that there seems little question that this was one of Zarathustra's original teachings. According to the *Vendidad*, the cultivation of the earth was looked upon by his followers as a kind of worship, a religious obligation. Among the sites where the earth feels most joyful is "the place where one of the faithful cultivates the most grain, grass, and fruit...where he waters ground that is dry or dries ground that is too wet." (*Vendidad* III.1.4) A little later in the same text (III.3.30-31), in answer to the question of which activity fills the law of Mazda, we are told that "it is sowing grain again and again.... He who cultivates grain, cultivates righteousness, and promotes and nurtures... the religion with a hundred new dwelling places." In the words of a scholar whose interpretation of the *Gathas* is based on the essential continuity of the Younger Avesta with the Gathic hymns, "agriculture was the great question of orderly and religious life with the Zarathustrians."[152]

The Life of the Prophet

If Zarathustra's original teachings may be pieced together using information in the Younger Avesta as well as the *Gathas*, the details of his life are more difficult to untangle. In the legendary accounts that have accrued over the millennia, both northeast and northwest Iran lay claim to his birthplace, and today the allegiance of Zoroastrian scholars is divided between these two regions. All agree, however, that Zarathustra was originally a priest, trained in the religion he would seek to reform. He refers to himself in the *Gathas* as a *zaotar*, cognate with the Sanskrit *hotr*, a fully qualified priest (*Yasna* 33.6*). As one Avestan scholar notes, Zarathustra did not intend to be the founder of a new religion. Like other great spiritual leaders — the Buddha, Jesus, Mohammed — he introduced often revolutionary new ideas into an established religious framework, "transforming it in accordance with his own understanding of the nature of God and the purpose of creation."[45]

Tradition holds that at the age of thirty Zarathustra began experiencing spiritual visions and came to realize what was needed to restore order and harmony to the world. Failing to win converts among his own people, the prophet was forced to travel afar. In the *Gathas* he asks:

> "To what land to flee?...
> They thrust me from family and clan.
> The community with which I have kept company
> has not shown me hospitality,
> nor those who are the wicked rulers of the land." (Y. 46.1)

Zarathustra is believed to ultimately have found refuge in a community whose leader, "Vishtaspa," became both convert and patron (Y. 51.16-21; 53.1-2), providing the prophet a base from which his teachings could then be spread. Along with a deeply sincere search for truth, the *Gathas* convey a powerful missionary urge, growing out of Zarathustra's conviction that Ahura Mazda had given him a message for all mankind. (Y. 44.10) The bearers of that message went forth to "those who seek Truth in other lands." (Y. 42.6) In the Younger Avesta we find, in addition to recognizably Iranian place-names, the names of lands and peoples quite unknown to history, all of which are said to have been converted to the way of the prophet.[27]

---

*The Gathas form the heart of the Yasna ceremony (described below) and are numbered in the order of their recitation in this central Zoroastrian ritual, hereafter abbreviated in Gathic references as "Y."

The Teachings of Zarathustra

The Zoroastrian religion is associated with a radical dualism which, however exaggerated it may have become over time, is believed to have originated with Zarathustra himself. According to one scholar, "the center of the religion evidenced by the *Gathas* was the opposition and conflict between day and night, light and darkness, order and deceit."[206] Some find the main elements of this dualism embodied in the opposition between Spenta Mainyu, the "bounteous spirit" identified with Ahura Mazda, and Angra Mainyu (later shortened to Ahriman), the "hostile spirit."[201] Others place the source of dualism in the contrast between *asha* (the principle of right order, associated, like Ahura Mazda, with truth and light) and *drug* (false order, deceit, darkness).[111] In any case, and in spite of the dualistic emphasis, the religion of Zarathustra is believed to have been essentially monotheistic, with Ahura Mazda as the sole creator god — a distinct contrast to the polytheism of the *Rigveda*.

It is important to note that the Zoroastrian concept of dualism cuts across both the material and the spiritual worlds, and is therefore not to be confused with the Gnostic dualism of matter and spirit in which spirit is identified with the divine.[200] The world created by Ahura Mazda, although under assault by the forces of evil, is inherently good. Zoroastrians subscribe to what one scholar calls a "cosmic dualism," in which the whole cosmos is permeated by a fundamental tension between the powers of good and evil, light and dark.[161] This opposition, which is expressed on every level of existence, had its origin in the *Gathas*:

> "Truly there are two primal Spirits,
> twins, renowned to be in conflict.
> In thought and word and deed they are two,
> the good and the evil." (Y. 30.3)

Each of these primal beings, presumably Ahura Mazda (or Spenta Mainyu) and the Hostile Spirit (Angra Mainyu), made a deliberate choice, according to his own nature, between good and evil. Ahura Mazda then created all things, first in spirit *(menog)* and then in material form *(getig)*, both perfect states of being. He began with the sky, traditionally conceived as a hard shell of crystal, and enclosed within it the other creations: water, earth, the archetypal plant, the "uniquely created bull," the first man, and fire. All was motionless and unchanging in this perfect creation, with the sun standing still overhead, as at noon.

The Hostile Spirit then broke through the sky and rushed upon the creations, bringing decay and corruption into the pure and supremely static world created by Ahura Mazda. The evil adversary turned much of the water to salt, made deserts on the earth, caused the plant to wither, and slew the bull and the man. The Amesha Spentas, spiritual emanations of Ahura Mazda (see below), then went into action, pressing the plant in the sacred mortar and pestle, and scattering its remains over the world. The seed of the bull and the man were likewise spread, giving rise to all the various animals and men. The cycle of earthly existence was thus set in motion, and the sun began to move across the sky, regulating the four seasons.[27, 29]

As told by the eminent British Zoroastrian scholar, Mary Boyce: "Ahura Mazda knew in his wisdom that if he became Creator and fashioned this world, then the Hostile Spirit would attack it, because it was good, and it would become a battleground for their two forces; and in the end he, God, would win the great struggle there and be able to destroy evil, and so achieve a universe which would be wholly good forever."[27] Because the battle between good and evil takes place in time, it is not unending, and the physical world has a crucial part to play in securing the ultimate outcome: the restoration of the earth to its original state of perfection.

All of the "creations" and time itself are therefore participants in the ongoing contest between the forces of light and darkness. Once the Hostile Spirit spread evil throughout the world, each realm — not only plants, animals and men, but also minerals, fire, and water — began to strive, consciously or unconsciously, to free itself from evil and regain its original state of purity.[28] Through this incessant conflict between light and darkness, the world is moving towards that final state, the "making glorious" or "renewal" of the earth, the *fraso-kereti*. At that moment, time and change will come to an end, and the kingdom of Ahura Mazda will be established on earth.

Zarathustra's concept of time is therefore cyclical in the sense that the world achieves once again the purity of its beginning, but this is not the cycle of an Eternal Return. The struggle to eradicate evil, the battle between Ahura Mazda and Ahriman, would go on and on, but it would not last forever.* In the Zoroastrian concept, there is no unending recurrence of events, but rather what Mary Boyce described as "a linear development to a once-more changeless state."[27] In contrast to the *Rigveda*, where the divinely appointed order is frequently disturbed but remains essentially as it has always been, static and unchanging, Zarathustra taught that once evil entered the world, nothing thereafter was still. In the words of another scholar, "Time itself was in motion, it was moving forward."[46]

Assisting Ahura Mazda in his efforts to overcome evil were the Amesha Spentas ("Holy Immortals"), entities perceived by Zarathustra as both emanations of Ahura Mazda's creative nature and spiritual guardians of the physical world. For example, Asha Vahishta, the spirit of the right order (*asha*) that pervades and regulates the world, is both the guardian of and immanent in the element of fire — not only the hearthfire but also the fiery sun that orders and regulates the seasons. The other five Amesha Spentas and the creations they protect are Vohu Manah, "good thought," protector of cattle (the animal kingdom); Khshathra, "dominion" or "sovereign power," the mineral realm; Haurvatat, "immortality," water; Ameretat, "wholeness or integrity," plants; and Armaiti, "devotion" or "humility," the protectress of farmers and herdsmen and often identified with the Earth. These associations, subtly alluded to in the *Gathas*, are clearly set out in the later literature.[28]

Through his conception of the Amesha Spentas, Zarathustra was able to weave together matter and spirit so that, as one scholar put it, "the physical world itself — or rather whatever was good and wholesome in the physical world — was seen as impregnated with moral purpose and directed by spiritual striving."[46] Of supreme importance in this effort was the conscious activity of man (i.e., mankind; women are of equal stature

---

Zoroastrians believe that at the end of time a saviour (saoshyant) will lead humanity in the final battle against evil, after which each individual will be judged by the goodness of his thoughts, words, and deeds. A flood of molten metal will burn up the last vestiges of evil, leaving the good unharmed and residing forever in the paradise of a perfect world.[29] The similarity of Zoroastrian eschatology to that of Judaism, Christianity, and Islam will be further explored in the epilogue.

with men in the Gathic hymns [Y. 35.6; 41.2; 37.3; 39.2]). He is the chief of the creations, bound to the others by the link of a common goal, "for all were brought into existence for this one end, namely the utter defeat of evil."[27] In working to expand the power of good over evil, man is expected to assist the other creations — plants, animals, minerals, etc. — in their own struggle for perfection.[234]

Everyday life thus presented Zarathustra's followers with an abundance of opportunities for putting their beliefs into practice, not only through the careful tending of their plants and animals, but also by guarding the purity of the water in springs and streams.[28] Reverence for water is almost as strong among Zoroastrians as the reverence for fire; an Avestan hymn worships the waters as the "wives of Ahura." The waters are addressed similarly in the *Rigveda* (as the "wives of Varuna"), suggesting that this symbolic association belonged to the archaic Indo-Iranian religion from which both traditions emerged.

Right Order

In forming his own worldview, Zarathustra seems to have incorporated several other principles of the ancient religion that he once served. Among these was the concept, mentioned earlier, of a universal right order (Avestan *asha*, Vedic *rta*).* At once cosmic, liturgical, and moral, this ordering principle was held to govern every aspect of existence, from the rhythms of the cosmos and the workings of nature to the conduct of man.[29] In Iran the righteous man was *ashavan*, possessing *asha*, an upholder of the right order of things. Zarathustra himself would claim to have seen into that order, vowing "while I have power and strength, I shall teach men

---

Although rta, *a term that appears several hundred times in the* Rigveda, *is generally equated with the Iranian* asha, rta *was essentially distinct from the gods, whereas* asha *is held to emanate directly from Ahura Mazda. In Vedic religion a "merely philosophical" distinction is made between order (*rta*) and chaos (*nirrti*), and in the Hindu world* rta *was gradually replaced by the concept of* dharma. *For Zoroastrians, however, the difference between* asha *and* drug *(false order) is an ethical one, and its significance has remained undiminished.*[45]

to seek the Right [asha]." (Y. 28.4) According to one scholar, asha is both the principle by which Zoroastrians guide their lives in this world and the basis on which the entire structure of the Zoroastrian faith rests: "The highest value in human life is neither the attainment of happiness nor the achievement of peace but the incessant work of spreading the ideal of righteousness [asha]."[161]

In the famous Gatha of the Choice, the individual is urged to choose for himself either the path of asha or the path of drug:

"Hear with your ears the highest truths I preach
And with illumined minds weigh them with care
Before you choose which of two paths to tread,
Deciding man by man, each one for each." (Y. 30.2-4)

The prophet is here urging all those who receive his message to judge for themselves, without clerical intermediary, the truth of his teaching. Just as the two primal beings each made a deliberate choice, so must every man choose — freely and without priestly intervention — between good and evil in this life. Zarathustra is believed to have been the first to teach that each individual must bear the responsibility for the fate of his own soul, as well as sharing in the responsibility for the fate of the world.[27] From the time of the Gathas onward, the task of the righteous man was to cherish and husband the created world, the "Good Creation."[46] As told by one authority, the actions of each individual would determine whether he belonged to the god of light or the demon of darkness. He stands by the former — and is a man of Asha — if he "enlarges the world of Ahura Mazda by spreading life over the world."[48]

The Transformation of Priests and Warriors

Zarathustra's encouragement of unmediated free choice is likely to have further alienated him from the priests of the old tradition. Religious corruption was apparently widespread in his time, with once-sacred rituals degenerating into drunken and lawless behavior.[45] It is therefore not surprising to find the role of the priest radically altered in Zarathustra's reforms, and religious observances primarily contained within the individual household.[28] Among his many innovations was the establishment of what one scholar envisioned as "a preaching vocation of all believers (*ashavans*)."[45] As we will see later, Zarathustra is also credited with the founding of the order of the Magi, in historical times a hereditary priesthood associated with western Iran.

In the early days of the religion, his disciples are likely to have been found on the road, in the fields, or both. As noted earlier, Zarathustra's reform was vigorously missionary in spirit, committed to *page 58* bringing the word of Ahura Mazda to all humanity. If, as indicated in the Younger Avesta, the agricultural way of life was an important part of that message, his representatives would have been as well-versed in plant and animal husbandry as in religious dogma. Irrigation, fertilization, and cattle breeding may all have been part of a missionary's wisdom. They may also have been architects and builders, if one early Zoroastrian scholar's picture of the movement as a whole is correct: "With the spread of the new doctrine, the increase in settlements goes hand in hand. When a hitherto nomadic tribe becomes converted to the Zoroastrian religion, it abandons its former unsettled mode of living, builds permanent dwellings, and cultivates the fields."[76]

While many scholars believe that the main issue facing Zarathustra was the struggle between agricultural and nomadic ways of life, others find suggestions of a falling out between priests of the old religion and bands of warriors who no longer accepted their authority.[126] Indications can be found in the *Gathas* (Y. 32.12-14; 44.20; 48.10; 49.4) that Zarathustra opposed not only the corrupt religious leaders of his time, but also groups of warriors who wantonly sacrificed cattle and excessively consumed the sacred intoxicant (Avestan *haoma*, Vedic *soma*).* Typical of Indo-Iranian culture were bands of young men who worshipped a war-god and revered

---

* *The botanical identity of the plant source for the Indo-Iranian* soma/haoma *(which simply means "that which is pressed") is unknown.*[192] *Its proper use was in ceremonial contexts, as part of a ritual offering prepared from the juice obtained by pounding or "pressing" the stems of the plant with a ceremonial mortar and pestle.*[27] *Although the pressing of the* haoma *would become one of the most important rites of the later Zoroastrian tradition, it has been suggested that this archaic Indo-Iranian practice was temporarily banned by Zarathustra, whose condemnation is believed to have been aimed primarily at the abuse, rather than the traditional use, of the* haoma.[59]

the spirits of ancestral warriors. They were known for intentionally cultivating a state of fury, drinking the sacred intoxicant and devouring great quantities of meat to attain physical strength.[126] We will later find that the main activity of these bands of "warriors" was actually cattle raiding, for which an archaic Indo-European myth provided justification and support.

Some observers feel that one of the most difficult aspects of Zarathustra's reform would have been the abolition of the warrior function as such, and the transformation of the man of arms into a "purified crusader in the service of the true religion."[61] For Vedic peoples the favorite of all gods was Indra, pictured in the *Rigveda* as a virile, strife-provoking warrior, drunk on songs and *soma* and bountiful to his followers, from whom he demanded abundant offerings. (RV IV. 42) Indra is not mentioned in the *Gathas*, but in the Younger Avesta he is reviled as a *daeva*, a term that means "god" (*deva*) in the *Rigveda* but "demon" in Avestan.[27]

Turning names of deities into names of demons is considered to be typical of a change of religion; the gods of the old religion become the demons of the new, as did the pagan deities in popular Christian tradition. In the opinion of one authority, "It was no doubt the rise of Zoroastrianism in the Iranian world that occasioned the linguistic and cultural split between the Iranian and Indian areas."[123] Other Zoroastrian scholars believe that the separation of Iranian from Indian preceded the appearance of Zarathustra.[26] Needless to say, dating the prophet to the seventh millennium would require a fresh look at the timing of the Indo-Iranian split.

The Yasna Ceremony

This brief survey of Zarathustra's teachings leaves no room for exploring the subtlety of his vision. As our investigation represents only a first step in rethinking the prophet's placement in time, we are necessarily limited, as we were in our overview of Neolithic archaeology, to the major themes defined by scholarly inquiry. The Zoroastrian religion is immensely more complex than its description here, and readers who want a further accounting are encouraged to consult the bibliography. For now, and before comparing Zarathustra's teachings with late-seventh-millennium archaeology, we will look at one final, particularly archaic tradition, the *yasna* ceremony.

The highest liturgy within the Zoroastrian religion today, the *yasna* ("sacrifice" or "act of worship") is believed to date back, in some form, to the period of Indo-Iranian unity. After the separation of the two peoples, the ceremony seems to have developed differently among Indians and Iranians,[26] but a comparison of the Zoroastrian ritual with the Vedic *yajna* has allowed a reconstruction of the ceremony as it is likely to have been observed in the period following Zarathustra's reform.

No altars, temples, or artificial icons would have been present, for the object of veneration was the world itself, both its material forms and the spiritual forces that suffused those forms.[28] Each of the seven creations would have been represented, thus insuring the presence of the Amesha Spentas as well. Earth was present in the ritual precinct (a small rectangle of clean ground); the "stone" of the sky was represented by the sacred mortar and pestle in which the *haoma*, representative of the plant creation, was pressed. The animal creation was represented by either a sacrificial beast or its products. (A saucer of goat's milk was customary in historical times.) Water was present in a libation vessel, fire in the ceremonial hearth, and the seventh creation, man, was represented by the celebrant. Offerings would have been made to each of the creations, which, through their participation in the *yasna*, were believed to be purified and strengthened in their ongoing struggle against the evil spirit.

The ceremony appears to have been of great importance to Zarathustra, who believed that the spiritual *yasna* performed by Ahura Mazda at the moment of creation would be reenacted at the end of time, the *fraso-kereti*.[26] At some point the prophet apparently taught his Gathic hymns to those disciples who celebrated the *yasna*, after which time these hymns were recited each day within the ceremony itself. Over the centuries additional prayers and hymns were apparently added, and today the *yasna* contains seventy-two chapters of text, at the heart of which remain the *Gathas*. According to observers of a contemporary *yasna*, the seventy-two chapters are still recited from memory in the Avestan tongue.[45]

At prescribed moments in the ceremony, the Zoroastrian priest unties and reties a sacred cord worn around the waist, a practice observed by lay worshippers in their own daily prayers.* When pressing the *haoma*, the priest vigorously pounds the plant twigs, striking the mortar with the pestle: "In so doing, he dramatically joins the cosmic battle between the forces of good and evil, each blow of the pestle smiting the invoked presence of Angra Mainyu (the evil one), the demon of wrath."[236] Participants of the *yasna* are thus placed directly within the context of the cosmic struggle between light and darkness.

Reflected within the Zoroastrian *yasna* is the essential unity of the creation of the world and the final goal toward which it is moving, the *fraso-kereti*. In the words of one scholar:

> "There is perhaps no other religion in which the beginning and the end of the world are so closely held together.... Creation in the Zoroastrian theology has no other aim but to lead towards eschatology; eschatology has no meaning but as completing the work of creation, and both taken together are two crucial stages in the battle against evil."[199]

Daily celebration of the *yasna* both anticipates the *fraso-kereti* and, in a sense, is expected to bring it about. The relationship between man and the divine beings is reaffirmed and strengthened, as is the responsibility of man to uphold the principles of right order *(asha)*. In Vedic society, individuals could indirectly help sustain the order of the world by contributing to the offerings that priests made to the gods, but the follower of Zarathustra is personally engaged in the struggle to promote *asha*: "His or her obligations permeate the whole of life."[46] Although all of Ahura Mazda's creations are felt to be interconnected parts of a whole, the activity of man is vital

---

* *Traditionally woven from sheep's wool and wrapped three times around the waist, the sacred belt or cord* (kushti) *worn by Zoroastrians apparently goes back to Indo-Iranian times. Hindus wear the cord, which is permanently knotted by a priest, over one shoulder, but Zarathustra is believed to have instructed his followers to wear it belted around the waist, and to untie and retie it themselves while standing in prayer.* [28]

to the well-being of the others, and his life is to be lived, according to another observer, with a sense of stewardship for all aspects of the Good Creation.[28] His prayer, voiced by Zarathustra in one of the *Gathas* and thus repeated daily in the *yasna:* "May we be those who shall renew this existence." (Y. 30.9)

The age of the *yasna* ceremony is unknown. Scholarly research has shown that rituals in particular, which tend to be faithfully repeated and defended against change, can achieve a remarkable continuity across vast stretches of time.[236] If Zarathustra lived in the seventh millennium, the roots of the Zoroastrian *yasna* would be of equal antiquity, and the Indo-Iranian tradition from which it derives would reach back even further into prehistory. The plausibility of such an enduring continuity will be explored in the next chapter, as we compare our earlier investigation of Late Neolithic archaeology with what we now know about Zarathustra and the religion that sprang from his teachings.

CHAPTER SIX

Convergences I:
Late Neolithic Archaeology
and Zoroastrian Traditions

"O Maker of the material world, thou Holy One!
　　What fulfills the law of Mazda?"
"It is sowing grain again and again....
　When the grain is coming forth, then faint the
　　daevas hearts;
　when the grain is being ground, the *daevas* groan;
　when wheat is coming forth, the *daevas* are destroyed."

　　　　　　　　　– Zend-Avesta, Vendidad III.3.30-32

Before examining the ways in which mid-to-late seventh millennium archaeology may support the ancient historians' placement of Zarathustra, a word should be said about the difficulties archaeologists face in precisely dating events of this early period. Problems with carbon-14 readings are often compounded by uncertainties about the context to which the carbonized test material actually belongs.[91] More important, carbon-14 dates carry a margin of error, usually between one and two hundred years, even after they have been corrected or "calibrated." The calibrated date used most frequently by archaeologists to mark the start of this new epoch, c. 6500 BC, is therefore still a relatively imprecise estimation of true calendar time. The same must be said for the various dates given by the Greek and Roman historians for the time of Zarathustra—c. 6480, 6350, and 6200 BC. In each of these claims, the number of years prior to a known historical event had clearly been rounded off (e.g., 6,000

page 54

years before the death of Plato, 5,000 years before the Trojan War). We therefore may never be able to establish a more precise correlation between these two sets of dates, ancient and modern, than that which already exists — and which already is quite remarkable.

We have observed the multitude of new farming settlements that spread across Iran, Iraq, and into southeast Europe in the last half of the seventh millennium BC. The painted patterns on their fine ceramics suggest a shared — and from the artistic excellence of many of these pieces, one might even say an inspired — symbolic tradition. We have considered Jacques Cauvin's suggestion that the spread of agriculture might everywhere have been accompanied by a new religion.[37] And we *page 37* have been informed by the *Zend-Avesta* that Zarathustra's missionaries *page 58* went forth to spread his word not only to Iranians but also to those who sought truth in other lands. An Avestan scholar's description of *page 64* the probable result of these missionary efforts has also been presented: "With the spread of the new doctrine, the increase in settlements goes hand in hand. When a hitherto nomadic tribe becomes converted to the Zoroastrian religion, it abandons its former unsettled mode of living, builds permanent dwellings, and cultivates the fields."[76] Although Wilhelm Geiger wrote that passage more than a hundred years ago, working only from his interpretation of the Avesta, it now bears a striking resemblance to the archaeological events of the mid-to-late seventh millennium BC.

We briefly followed the debate over the identity of the first *page 35ff* farmers of Greece, which has led to a consensus among scholars that both immigrants and indigenous peoples were involved in the settling of southeast Europe. Preliminary mitochondrial DNA findings suggested that the spread of agriculture across Greece and the Balkans was accomplished by farmers from abroad in combination with the conversion of local populations. If these migrating farmers were responding to *page 63* Zarathustra's agricultural imperative and "spreading life over the world," the determination that fueled the difficult voyage to Greece — and the subsequent transformation of local hunter-gatherers into husbandmen — could more readily be explained. (We will later find that following the way of *asha* in Greece and elsewhere may not necessarily have required the renunciation of indigenous religious traditions.)

Similar genetic studies are unavailable for the Middle East, but the choice of site locations throughout Iraq and Iran accentuates the uniqueness of this sweeping cultural change. Almost all of these new settlements were not only founded on virgin soil but were often located in previously unoccupied areas, some of which lie outside the rain-fed farming belt. The adoption of irrigation techniques, heretofore apparently *page 43* unknown, made these locations viable, but archaeologists remain puzzled as to why the founders of those new communities chose land that must be artificially watered. If they were indeed influenced by Zarathustra, those particular settlers may well have been acting on the belief, expressed in the *Vendidad*, that the earth rejoices not only where one of the faithful cultivates the most grain but also "where he waters ground that is dry." *page 57* In the view of a Zoroastrian scholar, irrigating the earth was "justly ranked among the first services of a human being."[152]

What is missing from these new settlements may be even more suggestive of Zarathustra's influence. Any explanation of the cultural changes that took place after c. 6500 BC must account for the virtual disappearance of the "cult inventory" associated with PPNB: human skulls, bulls' horns, and in particular the ornate weaponry that was often found buried with the dead. With the exception of Halaf (to be discussed later in more detail), the infrequent arrow and spear heads that appeared among the painted-pottery communities were present only in the lowest levels of newly founded sites and then disappeared entirely, leaving a preponderance of agricultural tools. Interpreters of the *Gathas* have told us that Zarathustra condemned the abusive practices of the warrior cults of his day, seeking, according to one, to transform these dissolute bands into "purified crusaders in the service of the true religion."[61] Might *page 65* the phasing out of elaborate weaponry after 6500 BC mean that such a transformation of the warrior had in fact been accomplished, at least in the painted pottery communities?

The presence of miniature mortars and pestles, if not symbolically related to the sacred implements used to ritually crush the *haoma* plant, serve as further evidence of the cultural commonality of new sites throughout Iran. On the Iranian plateau at Sialk, where the miniature *page 44* mortars and pestles were fashioned in clay as well as stone, excavators also uncovered an elegant knife handle carved in the form of a bowing male figure whose face is no longer intact (fig. 27). His knee-length garment is belted at the waist, and his hands and arms are described as "reverently folded across the front of the body in an attitude of obeisance which is already astonishingly Persian"[135] — an attitude depicting the traditional Iranian posture of greeting, more than three thousand years before Indo-Europeans are conventionally believed to have entered Iran.

Egalitarian Societies?

Settlement patterns show a striking similarity to one another in this period, and to what one would expect of Zarathustra's followers. According to an Avestan scholar, there would have been no distinction of occupation or class in Gathic communities,[28] an appropriately egalitarian arrangement for individuals urged in the *Gathas* to choose their own life's path, "each one for each." The immense size reached by PPNB sites in the previous period, some of which accommodated several thousand people, has suggested to observers that a form of hierarchical control may have been practiced in those earlier settlements. In contrast, the painted pottery villages were usually quite small, housing at most three hundred individuals. Working with population estimates in Early Neolithic Greece, Catherine Perlès concluded that Greek villages remained "under the threshold at which a pyramidal organization would have become necessary. No sign of institutionalized hierarchy, within or between the communities, is perceptible."[173] This apparently egalitarian pattern remained virtually unchanged for more than a thousand years in Greece, a long-term stability that Perlès feels may have been due to the rapid integration of local hunter-gatherers into the agricultural society.

An almost identical arrangement is revealed in northern Iraq, another region where more extensive excavating has allowed archaeologists to draw conclusions about settlement patterns and site size. Here excavators have found the social organization of the Halaf culture to have been characterized by a great many small and highly autonomous communities, initially organized at the family or household level. In the Balikh valley of northern Iraq, even the larger Halaf villages contained no more than fifty to one hundred people.[4] The Halafian founders of Umm Qseir in northeast Syria (map at fig. 17) were described as "pioneering farmsteaders" who had come to a previously uninhabited, marginal region with their domestic animals and plants.[242] As noted by another observer: "Whatever the origin of the Halafians, there is no evidence of brutal invasion; in fact all we know of them points to a slow infiltration of peaceful people who came to settle in regions that were then sparsely populated."[194] If the Halafians, whose culture emerged several centuries after the earliest painted pottery villages, were influenced by the ongoing missionary efforts of Zarathustra's followers, they, like other pioneers of this epoch, may have intentionally chosen to cultivate land that lay unsown, seeking to promote and nurture the religion "with a hundred new dwelling places." (*Vendidad* III.3.31)

Another significant departure from PPNB traditions was the virtual absence of recognizable religious structures among the painted pottery communities of both Greece and northern Iraq. We observed the elaborate ceremonial buildings of the preceding period; the "Skull Building" at PPNB Çayönü, with

Fig. 27
*Bone knife handle
from Sialk I (after
Ghirschman, 1938)*

its indications of blood sacrifice, comes particularly to mind. An page 21 excavator of Halafian sites has observed that, in contrast to the cult buildings common to PPNB, "the general picture for the Halaf period is one of a less public and more private ritual activity, hardly exceeding the limits of the individual household."[4] As mentioned earlier, the Zoroastrian religion is known for a scarcity of sacred architecture; its page 55 nucleus, according to Mary Boyce, lay not in the temple but in the individual household.[28] page 63

What little information we have from Iran suggests patterns of settlement similar to those of northern Iraq and Greece, and again a virtual absence of ceremonial architecture. The new Iranian farming villages seem to have rarely exceeded two hundred inhabitants,[138] and after the appearance of a "painted shrine" at the incompletely excavated site of Zaghe on the Iranian plateau,[158] which may have belonged to the preceding era, no certain religious structures dating to this period have been recovered in Iran. And yet the patterns painted on the ceramics of farming villages from the Middle East to the Aegean are clearly symbolic, almost certainly expressing religious or other ideological principles.

Deciphering the Pottery Symbols

As noted earlier, the absence of any indication that the fine pottery of this period was used for cooking or storage has led excavators to the conclusion that these ceramics probably served ritual purposes. But while there seems little doubt that their painted patterns were symbolic in nature, the actual meaning of those symbols in this Late Neolithic context has yet to be deciphered. One team of investigators has laid the foundation for such an effort by identifying the designs on the richly patterned surfaces of the Iranian vessels as a kind of coded information. In the view of these scholars, "the complex patterns covering almost the entire surface of bowls and jars became an instrument for representing and transmitting an ideological heritage common to very large areas."[213]

page 32

If the development and diffusion of Zarathustra's original vision was indeed taking place in the centuries after 6500 BC, the ideological heritage that these analysts found represented on the painted surfaces of the pottery of this period would very likely have reflected his teachings. In perhaps the most obvious correlation, the dualism for which the Zoroastrian religion is known — the opposition between the forces of light and darkness — would have been well depicted by the patterns based on light and dark triangles and checkerboard designs that appeared on ceramics from Iran to Greece (figs. 16, 21e, 23). The double-axe motif that was widely applied to the pottery of this period (e.g., fig. 20) is also associated with the duality of opposing forces.[43] The effort made by potters to achieve maximum contrast between dark and light in their ceramic designs — many of which were based on variations of the double-axe — would further have emphasized these dualistic themes. In fact, the fields of intricate light-dark patterning on

page 49

both Halafian and Samarran pottery are particularly reminiscent of the Zoroastrian "cosmic dualism," in which, as described earlier, the whole *page 59* cosmos is permeated by the fundamental tension between good and evil, light and dark.

In addition to purely geometric designs, the pottery of Iran (Cheshmeh Ali style) and Iraq (Samarran, Halafian) was occasionally graced by motifs from nature — plants (reeds, trees, flowers), animals (ibex, leopard, bull), and stylized human figures — which may have evoked either the "creations" of Ahura Mazda or the Amesha Spentas *page 61* who dwelled within and protected each. (The recognizably female figures, for example, if not local goddesses, could have symbolized Armaiti, the Amesha Spenta often identified with the Earth.) We might then expect to find the other creations — water and fire — also represented on the pottery, perhaps among the numerous geometric motifs.

Outstanding among the ceramic patterns of this period were combinations of cross and circle, often referred to as "wheels" or "wheeled-cross" designs (figs. 19, 21d, 22). Scholars of ancient symbolism tell us that "from the very earliest times, the circle was used to express fullness and perfection."[43] As the cross is known to have traditionally been associated with the earth itself, these static wheeled-cross patterns might have represented the perfection of the world, either at the Zoroastrian moment of creation or at the end of time, the *fraso-kereti*. On both occasions, which together form a unity in Zoroastrian *page 67* theology, the earth is said to be motionless, with the sun standing overhead, as at high noon.

In contrast, motifs that emphasize movement, in particular the ubiquitous "whirl patterns" (figs. 18b, 21c), might illustrate Zarathustra's revelation that once evil entered the world, everything was set in motion; *page 60* the sun began to move across the sky, regulating the four seasons. His further belief that the earth itself is moving toward a higher goal might then be reflected in the spiral patterns of this period (fig. 21b).

The same analysts who theorized that the symbols painted on these ceramic surfaces represented encoded ideological information observed that the pottery bearing those symbols was distributed over a very large geographical area.[213] In fact, the question of why many of the finest of these ceramics were carried across great distances has long puzzled archaeologists. Halaf pottery, for example, has been shown by neutron activation to have been present in settlements whose distance from one another is more than six hundred miles.[68] The Halafians themselves were described by another scholar as having "peacefully invaded a wide area and mingled with the local population."[194] Might the Halafians have been using their extraordinary works of ceramic art as a means of spreading the word of the prophet?

page 50

If the finest of these ceramics were in fact reserved for ritual use, our question regarding the age of the *yasna* ceremony may be appropriately addressed here as well. At the end of the last chapter, we asked if some version of the Zoroastrian *yasna* might already have been practiced in the late seventh or early sixth millennium BC. In favor of this suggestion stand the variously shaped and painted, non-culinary ceramics of this period (fig. 28), any of which could have been used as containers for the offerings made during the *yasna*. And if the wheeled-cross, spiral, and whirl patterns carried the meanings suggested above, they might well have served as illustrative reinforcements of Zarathustra's teachings within the context of this ceremony. Both the story of the creation and the goal toward which the world is moving are evoked in the Zoroastrian *yasna*, which has been described as "a ceremony replete with eschatological meaning and potential."[45]

page 66

page 67

A great deal more work is needed on the interpretation of pottery symbols in this period. Our attempt to decipher the wheeled-cross and whirl patterns is only a beginning, and it is perhaps more important at this point to observe that whatever their meaning, the appearance of these patterns on the ceramics of peoples from the Iranian plateau to Greece (map at fig. 29) clearly demonstrates the cultural ties that were already present in the earliest of the new farming settlements that spread across

Fig. 28 Selected shapes, Cheshmeh Ali style ceramics (after Maleki, 1968)

these lands. As we will see below, this sweeping agricultural movement seems likely to have been accompanied by not only a new religion, but a new world order as well.

The Ubiquity of *Asha*

We earlier observed the displacement of Halaf in the fifth millennium by 'Ubaid, an expanding culture that was apparently indigenous to *page 51* southernmost Iraq.[157] Although many scholars see the 'Ubaid tradition, which offers the first known temple architecture, as a precursor of the Sumerian civilization, the pottery of 'Ubaid is said to be distinctly inferior to Halafian ceramics, with a monotony of designs that "betrays a lack of imagination."[194] And yet 'Ubaid ware is believed to ultimately have been derived from the excellent Samarra-related ceramics found at base levels of Eridu c. 6300 BC, the earliest known settlement *page 43* in southern Iraq. If, as suggested earlier, Eridu was among the new settlements called into being by Zarathustra's agricultural imperative, how could the subsequent, apparently continuous, cultural sequence in southern Iraq lead to the non-Indo-European (and distinctly non-Zoroastrian) Sumerian civilization?

We earlier cited Joan Oates' conclusion that a number of different ethnic groups were probably represented among the founders of the Middle Eastern painted pottery communities, various indigenous *page 44* peoples who may originally have been hunters, food-gatherers, or nomadic herdsmen. Persian texts indicate that missionaries bearing Zarathustra's message went forth to other lands, converting non-Aryans *page 58* (non-Indo-Europeans) as well as Aryans to the way of the prophet. If the c. 6300 BC founding of Eridu was indeed a non-Aryan response to Zarathustra's imperative, the people of southern Iraq may initially have embraced his religious teachings before later reverting to their former (pre-Sumerian) traditions.

It is also possible that new farmers here and elsewhere continued to practice their own religion while at the same time adopting a settled agricultural way of life—particularly if their worldview already included a concept similar to Zarathustra's *asha*. This principle of a universal order, governing the conduct of men as well as the rhythms of the *page 62*

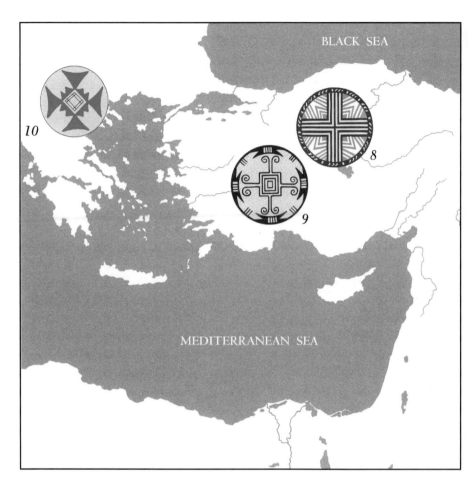

Fig. 29 *The distribution of wheeled-cross and whirl patterns on ceramics recovered from: 1 Karatepe,*

cosmos, was very widely spread in the ancient world, appearing not only among Indo-European peoples (Avestan *asha,* Vedic *rta*), but in Egypt (*maat*) and China (*tao*) as well.[66] Sumerian religion also included the idea of a world order, which was maintained through the performance of archaic rites.[194]

The age of this ubiquitous concept is unknown, but if the beliefs of the indigenous nomadic populations of southern Iraq and elsewhere already included such a principle in the seventh millennium

2 Ismailabad, 3 Eridu, 4 Tell es-Sawwan, 5 Hassuna, 6&7 Arpachiyah, 8&9 Hacilar, 10 Sesklo

BC, the adoption of agriculture may not have required the renunciation of their own religion. If their leaders were persuaded that the world order had changed, that it now lay in cultivating the earth, the shift to settled farming could have been accomplished without violating their core beliefs. As we will see later, the religious freedom that Cyrus the Great allowed the various ethnic groups within the (officially Zoroastrian) Persian Empire of the first millennium BC was both critical to the success of his reign and a tribute to Zarathustra's doctrine of free choice.

Questions of Identity

If the archaeology of the Neolithic Middle East can plausibly be compared to the traditions surrounding Zarathustra, we must then ask if the hymns known today as the *Gathas* and attributed to the prophet himself could have been composed in the seventh millennium BC. The difficulty of determining when material that has been carried in the oral tradition was actually created has been acknowledged, as has the fact that the *Gathas* are considerably more ancient than even the Younger Avesta, which, contrary to its name, is itself extremely old. Still, it seems hard to believe that the Gathic hymns could have been preserved in the oral tradition for more than 6,000 years, prior to being written down early in the Christian era.

page 55

On the other hand, it is possible that Zarathustra's hymns went through a continuous process of paraphrase and "translation" over time. In the view of one scholar, the archaic and impenetrable language of the *Gathas* in their present form may actually represent only the final stage at which the text was fixed when the language became too incomprehensible to be further changed. In his opinion: "Several stages of transmission no doubt already lay behind it." [234]

Related to this question, perhaps, is the recent suggestion that the *Gathas* are not the work of a single individual. The numerous times that Zarathustra refers to himself by name in these hymns (Y. 28.7, 29.8, 33.14, 50.6) has contributed to the theory that the *Gathas* represent the expression of a group rather than one man, and could have been written by any of those in the "Gathic circle." [111] As yet this idea has received little support, but if Zarathustra lived in the seventh millennium, a great many people would have been involved, not in the creation but in the transmission of the *Gathas* over time. The many third-person references to Zarathustra in hymns that he himself originally composed might therefore have arisen during multiple paraphrasings and updatings of the *Gathas* by his followers over the millennia.

It is also possible that there was more than one "Zarathustra." A much-disputed passage in the Avesta (Y.19.18) mentions four masters — of house, village, tribe, province — and a fifth and uppermost who was given the title *zarathustrotema*, "the one most like Zarathustra." [28]

Other translations of this term as "high priest" and "greatest or highest Zarathustra" contribute to the impression that the name "Zarathustra" may have become a priestly title, a generic term given to leaders of the religion he founded. According to one interpreter, "his name, entirely apart from all family connection, may have become a title for leading politico-ecclesiastical officials."[152]

It is interesting to note that the one place in which the master of the province was also the *zarathustrotema* was said to be "Ragha," believed by many scholars to be ancient Raga (modern Rayy),[105a] which lies directly adjacent to the old mound of Cheshmeh Ali on the Iranian plateau. One authority interpreted this passage to mean that Ragha was "plainly the seat of the religious government."[108] Others concluded that Zarathustra himself was present at Ragha,[14] or that Ragha became "a stronghold of his descendants" who were traditionally called by his name.[152] We will return to this passage, and to the proximity of Raga to Cheshmeh Ali, when exploring questions of the homeland of Zarathustra and his place of refuge.

The use of the prophet's name by later heads of the Zoroastrian religion might also explain the occasional indications in ancient literature that there was more than one historical Zarathustra. Pliny, for example, when placing Zarathustra 6,000 years before the death of Plato, remarked that "it is not so clear whether there was only one man of this name, or another one later on."[177] The existence of more than one Zarathustra could also help to explain the difference in the dates assigned to the prophet, as well as the multiple claims to his place of birth and the conflicting views held by scholars regarding his historical milieu. At one extreme Zarathustra has been described as a primitive ecstatic, a kind of "shaman,"[163] while at the other he is depicted as the worldly familiar of kings and court politics.[96]

Social Hierarchy

One further word about the antiquity of the *Gathas*. As Mary Boyce points out, certain elements of the Gathic hymns appear to be not only *page 56* considerably older than the Younger Avesta but even more archaic than the *Rigveda* of India, to which, as we have seen, the *Gathas* are linguistically related.[28] For example, the language of the Gathic hymns (Old Avestan) has no terms for the social stratification associated with different callings (priest, warrior, farmer/herder), terms that are present in both the *Rigveda* and the Younger Avesta. Equally puzzling is the fact that the Vedic and the Young Avestan names for these callings are quite different from one another. (The term for priest, for example, is *brahman* in Vedic and *athravan* in Young Avestan.) We earlier quoted one scholar's observation that Zarathustra's hymns express a "radical change in religious ideas that looks like a revolution" with respect to the Indo-Iranian religion described in the *Rigveda*.[111] Is it then possible that one of Zarathustra's reforms of the Indo-Iranian religion was the removal of a social hierarchy that was later reinstated in the society of the Younger Avesta?

page 57

The egalitarian settlement patterns within the farming communities founded after c. 6500 BC have been described above. In contrast to the large and possibly hierarchically organized settlements of the preceding PPNB period, painted pottery villages from Greece to northeastern Iran typically housed fewer than three hundred people, with no evidence of institutionalized hierarchy. The ceremonial structures of PPNB, which some scholars found suggestive of the presence of priestly officiants, played no part in the painted pottery cultures, nor did the elaborate weapons that suggested a warrior tradition among PPNB peoples. The disappearance of these elements might mean that any distinctions of priest or warrior in PPNB culture were either abolished or radically transformed among the painted pottery communities. The absence of social hierarchy in the *Gathas* might therefore indicate that the egalitarianism implied by settlement patterns after 6500 BC was indeed one of the reforms initiated by Zarathustra. If so, the presence of class distinctions in the Younger Avesta would indicate the ultimate failure of this aspect of his teachings.

page 72

By now it will be obvious to the reader that if Zarathustra lived c. 6500 BC, the dissolute practices he condemned—and from which he broke away—most likely belonged to the late stages of the tradition archaeologists have named PPNB. In the next chapter we will further explore the similarities between PPNB culture and the Indo-Iranian society described in the *Rigveda*. At least one contemporary authority has claimed that the rise of Zoroastrianism was responsible for the cultural and linguistic separation of the Iranian and Indian peoples. Other

page 65

scholars disagree, partly because the Indo-Iranian split seems certain to have taken place before the date (c. 1500-1200 BC) that several have assigned to Zarathustra. But if the prophet lived when the ancient Greek and Roman historians said he did, his mid-seventh millennium reforms could theoretically have triggered the beginnings of the separation of Iranian from Indian, contributing, perhaps, to a major dispersal of the greater Indo-European language family to which both belong.

CHAPTER SEVEN

Convergences II:
Pre-Pottery Neolithic B
and Vedic Traditions

"By adapting the structure of the institution of the warrior
and superimposing upon it an ethical component, Zarathustra
was able to suggest that the real battle was the one against the
forces of evil, and the real prize would not be territory, or
even men and cattle, but the realization of the good dominion
(*khshathra*) of Ahura Mazda."

— Peter Clark, *Zoroastrianism*

To investigate the possibility that late PPNB represents the tradition
that Zarathustra sought to reform, we must venture further into the
background and content of the *Rigveda*, our main source of knowledge
about the Indo-Iranian religion whose excesses were denounced by the
prophet. Clearly the result of an immensely long oral transmission from
teacher to pupil, the hymns of the *Rigveda* are believed to have endured
a continuous process of updating and amending over the centuries.
But unlike Zarathustra's *Gathas,* the *Rigveda* is not considered to be the
creation of a single author or of any one moment in time. Scholars have
found numerous stages in the creating, collecting, and preserving of the
Vedic material, along with evidence that at some point—or points—the
received hymns were "homogenized."[52]

For our purposes, the date of the actual composing of the Vedic
hymns is not as important as the idea, expressed by several scholars, that
many Vedic images and themes—such as deities, archaic elements of

culture, reminiscences of bygone periods — were a great deal older than the formal compositions themselves.[33] If those archaic elements date back as far as the eighth millennium BC, the traditions described in the *Rigveda* could theoretically represent a continuation of practices we have observed in the PPNB culture of that period. Fortunately, and in contrast to the Gathic hymns, which are primarily concerned with the moral and spiritual teachings of the prophet, the *Rigveda* describes an actual way of life, pursued within a society that many see as typical not only of archaic Indo-Iranian culture but of the greater Indo-European tradition as a whole. This more mundane aspect of the *Rigveda* should therefore make it relatively easy to compare Vedic culture with the archaeology of PPNB.

Fig. 30 Obsidian spearpoint from late PPNB levels, Çatal Höyük, central Turkey (after Mellaart, 1964)

Several congruences present themselves immediately. The society pictured in the *Rigveda* demonstrated an inherent desire for conquest, glorified its warriors (both living and dead), and worshipped a war-god (Indra) who was often associated with the wild bull.[66] As we saw earlier, PPNB has also been referred to as a "conquering culture,"[37] with expansionist tendencies that are well-documented archaeologically. Its "love affair with weapons"[37] may well indicate the existence of a warrior tradition within PPNB society — although, as we will see later, the main activity of both PPNB and Vedic warriors may not have been the waging of war at all. Cauvin tells us that PPNB armaments "may be readily correlated with the importance of the wild cattle and with the presence of a masculine anthropomorphic God."[37] Furthermore, the frequent display of human skulls that were occasionally plastered and painted to resemble faces, together with the custom of burying fine weapons with the dead, suggests that PPNB peoples practiced a veneration of ancestors equal to that described in the *Rigveda*.

What is more, with the possible exception of Halaf, none of the painted pottery cultures of the mid-to-late seventh millennium retained more than occasional remnants of these traditions. While the presence of arrow and spear heads in the base levels of a few of the earliest new *page 40* farming villages suggests an initial connection to PPNB culture (as do the domesticated species and occasional red-plastered floors), the disappearance of projectile points in later levels of those sites implies a final break with the PPNB weapons tradition. The displays of human skulls associated with PPNB were nowhere in evidence among the early painted pottery cultures, nor were the elaborate ceremonial contexts in which many of the skulls had appeared. PPNB statuary of a god-like male figure associated with bulls disappeared as well.

But Vedic peoples were evidently nomadic pastoralists, while PPNB is the culture that introduced — and further developed — rectangular architecture. By the early seventh millennium, however, many of the permanent PPNB settlements had been abandoned, and some of the finest weapons of this culture were being crafted in the campsites of nomadic pastoralists *(see page 24)*. Is it possible that those nomadic peoples who were not converted to the teachings of Zarathustra continued to maintain "PPNB" traditions for thousands of years, enshrining those traditions in hymns that would become the *Rigveda*?

If so, while many of these nomadic pastoralists must subsequently have migrated to India, others might simply have retired to mountain strongholds located within the original range of PPNB culture. Linguists are still puzzled by the fact that the earliest inscriptional evidence of the Vedic language comes not from India but from northern Iraq. In the second millennium BC, a treaty was drawn up at Bogazköy in Turkey between the ruler of the Hittites and the king of the land of Mitanni (the northern part of Iraq and Syria), in which several Vedic gods were mentioned along with

Fig. 31 Flint knife or dagger with carved bone handle, Çatal Höyük (after Mellaart, 1967)

Mesopotamian divinities. Indo-European scholars have struggled for years with the question of how Vedic traditions could have traveled as far west as northern Iraq in 1400 BC.[20] It may be that they never left.

Ritual Observances

Even in smaller details the comparison between PPNB and Vedic culture is useful, and though each of the following convergences, taken by itself, is far from conclusive, the overall similarity is intriguing. With regard to burial customs, for example, most known PPNB burials were secondary, with the dead presumably exposed to the elements before the cleaned bones were placed beneath the floors of the living quarters. Vedic peoples are also known to have practiced secondary burial after exposure of the dead, based on the belief that the resurrection of the body would take place a year after death: "Then the clean dry bones would be clothed again in flesh, so that the spirit, once more embodied, could enjoy to the full the tangible delights of heaven."[28]

page 22 The burials of high-status PPNB individuals were accompanied not only by fine weaponry but often by miniature forms of the polished greenstone axes whose evident symbolic value was noted earlier. Classical scholars have recorded the traditional association of polished stone axes with Indo-European gods of thunderstorms,[25a, 47] and in the *Rigveda* the axe is the thunderbolt of Indra, felling trees as does lightning in the storm:

> "Grasping his thunderbolt with both hands,
> Indra made its edge most keen....
> Thou crashest down the trees,
> O Indra, as when a craftsman fells,
> crashest them down as with an axe." (RV I.80.4)

page 62 Although Vedic culture was essentially masculine in character, "the waters" were portrayed as feminine (the "Apas" or the "wives of Varuna"), which might explain the many small female figurines in PPNB sites. They are to be distinguished from the large, well-crafted female statuettes that appeared after 6500 BC at Çatal Höyük and elsewhere. These later figures are of various mien and show regional differences, suggesting that they may represent early forms of local goddess traditions (e.g., Kybele of Turkey).

The Vedic texts might also lead us to an understanding of the purpose of the primitive little clay containers that appeared at Çayönü *page 22* and other PPNB sites long before the advent of true pottery. References in the *Rigveda* to clay vessels produced without a pottery wheel could simply mean, as some have suggested, that the hymns themselves were composed outside the region in which pottery wheels came into use in the fourth millennium.[121] But other scholars have observed that even after the potter's wheel became known to Vedic peoples, hand-made clay containers were still prescribed for the ritual sphere. Furthermore, the Vedic ceremonial vessels were required to be of a distinctly *inferior* quality — porous, without any decoration or paint, and fired by a primitive baking method in a simple open pit.[33] Recalling the primitive clay containers of Çayönü, one wonders if their use might indeed have been ceremonial, as excavators suggested, and if the later insistence on using plain, poorly fired, clay receptacles in Vedic rituals was part of an intentional reenactment of archaic PPNB rites.

Fig. 32 Uniquely preserved carved wooden containers from Çatal Höyük Level VI (after Mellaart, 1964)

We have observed that the Skull Building at PPNB Çayönü was apparently the site of blood sacrifices, human as well as bovine. Both types of sacrifice were part of the Vedic tradition, accompanied, as were those at Çayönü, by a ritual flint knife. Çayönü's *page 21* excavators have suggested that the finely carved and conserved pestles also found at their site may have been used in preparing ceremonial food or drink, while in the *Rigveda* an entire hymn is dedicated to the "pressing stones," the mortar and pestle, with which the stalks of the *soma* plant were ground to extract the sacred juice.[166] If the wooden containers in which the *soma* juice was then traditionally offered to the gods were also used at Çayönü, they did not survive (but see examples of wooden containers preserved at Çatal Höyük, figure 32). Although Zarathustra seems to have denounced immoderate consumption of the sacred intoxicant in his own time, it presumably had been used with restraint in earlier phases of the Indo-Iranian religion.

Parallel with the prophet's denunciation of the abuse of intoxicants was his rebuke of crimes against cattle, crimes that are believed to have involved either excessive animal sacrifice, the stealing of cattle, or both.[27] The great number of bulls' horns adorning the chambers of the PPNB-related site of Çatal Höyük (e.g., fig. 35) could mean that the sacrifice of cattle had dramatically increased in the first half of the seventh millennium. Is it possible that the stealing of cattle — cattle raiding — was also practiced at this time?

Cattle and Cattle Raiders

After their separation, both Iranian and Indian peoples continued to place great importance on cattle. In the *Gathas* the term "cattle" represents all domestic animals (e.g., sheep and goats are "small cattle"), and one remarkable passage affirms both the symbolic importance of the cow and the closeness of man and animal in Zarathustran communities:[28]

> "We reverence the Soul and Maker of the cow;
> we reverence our own souls and (those) of domestic animals
> which seek refuge with us...." (Y. 39.1)

In Vedic traditions as well, the image of the cow was both pervasive and multivalent. But here, cattle were directly equated with wealth and eminence — "may we be famed among the folk for wealth in kine"(RV X. 64.11) — and the bull, as noted earlier, was symbolically supreme.[166]

In his investigation into Indo-European mythology, Bruce Lincoln concluded that the exalting of cattle may actually date back to the time of the Indo-European unity.[126] One well-known practice, the cattle raid, exemplifies the value placed on these animals. In the *Rigveda*, for example, the primary activity of the warrior is actually not the waging of war but the stealing of cattle, an activity that is glorified as a heroic undertaking throughout the Vedic hymns.[33] Using the mythological traditions of several Indo-European peoples — Greeks, Germans, Celts, Romans, Hittites, as well as Indo-Iranians — Lincoln has been able to reconstruct a proto-Indo-European myth of the first cattle raid. In it a heroic figure loses his cattle to a three-headed monster and is helped by a warrior god (Vedic: Indra) to recover the stolen herd. According to Lincoln, this myth provided Indo-European warrior societies with both the justification for stealing cattle in raids (recovering what originally belonged to the raiders) and the validation of cattle raiding as the proper activity of a true warrior (warfare becomes identified with the quest for cattle).[126]

Lincoln further believes that the practice of cattle raiding is actually as old as the keeping of cattle itself,[126] which would mean that these practices date back to the eighth millennium and the presence of domestic cattle in PPNB sites. If he is right and the stealing of cattle in raids is in fact as old as their domestication, the primary activity of late PPNB "warriors" may in fact have been cattle raiding. While there is little evidence of warfare in the PPNB period, small-scale cattle raids by mobile bands of men would have left few permanent traces.* Historically the relationship between settled farmers and nomadic peoples has often been fruitful, but it is not hard to imagine that relationship deteriorating along with the other signs of cultural breakdown in late PPNB.

While the Vedic poets sang of cattle raids as admirable operations, profitably carried out by brave and adventurous men,[28] Zarathustra held a different view. In the *Gathas* he speaks out against renegades who destroy the *pasu-vira*, the community of cattle and men. Gathering in bands, they devour what belongs to others and do harm to the life of the cow (Y. 32.12; 31:15). In another passage, the Soul of the Cow implores Ahura Mazda:

"Wrath and violence, harm, daring, and brutality have bound me!
I have no other pastor than you;
appear to me with good husbandry!" (Y. 29.1)

Most Zoroastrian scholars believe that this Gathic hymn is both metaphysical—an allegory for the suffering of the righteous man's soul in

---

Evidence of physical violence in the PPNB period is reported to be "scarce but not absent," with arrowheads occasionally found embedded in the skeletons of individuals at several different sites.[6]

its quest for "the good vision"—and descriptive of the reality of a cattle raid from the point of view of its victims, portraying "the brutal carrying off of hapless cattle."[28] As pictured by one authority: "Zarathustra, the Soul of the Cow, and the Ahuras represent a peace-loving, sedentary form of agriculture in which animal husbandry played an important role. Pitted against them are the wild, lawless nomads and persistent followers of the old ways, all worshippers of the Daevas."[130]

page 24 The reason for the widespread desertion of PPNB settlements in the late eighth and early seventh millennium continues to puzzle archaeologists. Following Bruce Lincoln's lead, it seems reasonable to suggest that some part of this unexplained site abandonment might have been due to an intensification of cattle raiding, which either demoralized the settlers or actually drove them from their villages. For example, cattle raids might have been the reason for the fortifying, and later the abandonment, of Tell Magzaliya (map at fig. 5), a late eighth millennium settlement in northern Iraq that yielded large numbers of PPNB-type arrowheads within the context of an agricultural community. Sheep and goats were herded from the start; domestic cattle were apparently introduced later. The keeping of cattle seems to have roughly coincided here with the construction, also late in the occupation, of a massive defensive wall that encircled the entire community. When these fortifications were discontinued at a still later time, the settlement at Tell Magzaliya was significantly diminished and soon was abandoned.[9]

Elsewhere in the late PPNB period, some settlers may have chosen to protect their herds by moving out of reach of the raiders. The difficulty of transporting cattle across the Mediterranean Sea was page 31 noted earlier, and yet domestic cattle were included in even the earliest Greek settlements, the handful of known sites that were founded before the massive explosion of settlement activity began there c. 6400 BC. The lack of a consistent cultural resemblance, beyond the domesticated species and a few random artifacts, between these earliest Greek settlements and known sites in the Near East suggested to one observer that "these pioneers were small groups of adventurous individuals, who did not carry, possess, or choose to retain the whole technical and cultural heritage of their original communities."[173]

We earlier noted the absence of PPNB arrow and spear heads in Greece, as well as any sign of "cult furniture." If the difficulty in tracing the earliest Greek farmers to a specific culture in the Near East is in fact the result of the new settlers' conscious desire to leave their former traditions behind, it seems possible that these first few migrating groups, whose early seventh millennium dates would precede the theorized influence of Zarathustra, had consciously chosen to distance themselves from the cult excesses of late PPNB — particularly if those practices had included the stealing of cattle. Several hundred years later, those who migrated to Greece from c. 6400 BC, our theoretical bearers of Zarathustra's teachings, may have found a few scattered groups, already established, that were sympathetic to his reforms.

Of the known Near Eastern sites from which those earliest Greek settlers might have emigrated, the largest — and ultimately the most clearly decadent — was the seventh millennium, PPNB-related center at Çatal Höyük (fig. 1), one of the main sites Colin Renfrew has used in theorizing a proto-Indo-European presence in Neolithic Turkey.[183, 184] A brief look back at this huge site, whose occupation preceded and then slightly overlapped the advent of the painted pottery cultures, will reveal in greater detail the suggested correspondence between PPNB and Vedic traditions.

Çatal Höyük, c. 7300 – c. 6300 BC: an Indo-European Stronghold?

Indo-European culture is traditionally associated with a tripartite social *page 82* system of priests, warriors, and husbandmen. In early Vedic society the high priest appears to have been in some measure the leader or ruler of the community.[28] Although many prehistorians have denied the existence of hierarchical social organization in the Neolithic period, the sheer size of the settlement at Çatal Höyük, which housed up to 7,000 people in peak periods, has convinced others that some form of social stratification must have been present.[173] Several of the stone figurines from the site depict robed, priest-like figures, one of which appears to be riding an animal (fig. 33). The abundance of religious iconography on the walls of the excavated portion of the site also suggested to James Mellaart, the original excavator of Çatal Höyük, that he had tapped into the "priests' quarter." Mellaart presumed that separate facilities for artisans and husbandmen existed elsewhere on the Çatal mound in what he believed to have been a stratified society of full-time specialists.[145]

The possibility that some of these artisans may actually have been members of a warrior tradition is suggested by the fact that one of the finest aesthetic endeavors at Çatal Höyük was the crafting of ornate weaponry. Before succumbing to the impoverishment typical of final

PPNB assemblages, flint and obsidian weapons reached new heights of elaboration at this site. The flint knives (fig. 31) accompanying prestigious male burials show remarkable skill, and the obsidian spear heads (fig. 30) that were frequently found buried, unused, with the dead have been deemed "easily the most elegant in the Near East."[145] Miniature greenstone axes also accompanied the dead, while larger ones were placed, possibly as offerings, in the shrine-like chambers above these burials. The presence in the *Rigveda* of plausible counterparts for each of these finely crafted implements invites us to more thoroughly explore the possibility that among the honored dead at Çatal Höyük were members of a warrior society resembling that described in the Vedic hymns.

We were earlier informed that PPNB-style weapons similar to those at Çatal Höyük can be correlated to both the presence of an anthropomorphic male god and the importance of cattle in PPNB culture.[37] The rather primitive, youthful male figure seated on a bull at figure 34

Fig. 33 Stone statuettes from Çatal Höyük VI.10 (after Mellaart, 1963)

could represent a prototype of Indra, the Vedic warrior god, and there is certainly no lack of bull symbolism within the Çatal chambers. Heads of bulls, molded from plaster but with actual horn cores, were often mounted on the surfaces of walls, and a "bull pillar," a single mud-brick topped with a bull's horns, became a popular icon in peak levels VII and VI. The extremes to which the fascination with cattle was carried at Çatal Höyük is perhaps best exemplified in the chamber depicted in figure 35, where a row of seven horn cores of *Bos primigenius* were set into a "bull bench" that was surely used for other than domestic purposes. The excavators have not ventured an interpretation of this construction, but if some part of the Çatal tradition was not only Indo-European but more specifically Indo-Iranian, the bull bench may actually have served as an initiation couch.

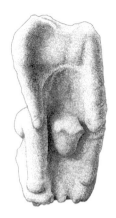

Fig. 34 Male figure on bull from Çatal Höyük VII.21 (after Mellaart, 1963)

According to Bruce Lincoln, an intense initiation was required for those who sought to join the ranks of the Indo-Iranian warrior bands, for the status of the warrior was "charged with magico-religious power and must be entered accordingly."[126] The close association of the Indo-Iranian warrior god with the bull suggests that the bull bench at Çatal Höyük may have provided this kind of experience to the novice. As Lincoln further observes: "In a certain sense initiation was also a ritual death and rebirth and served to introduce the novice to his celestial counterparts, the warriors of the dead."[126] As in other PPNB sites, human skulls were frequently displayed in Çatal chambers (e.g., fig. 36). Might they have belonged to deceased members of the warrior band the novices sought to join?

The initiatory themes of death and rebirth, and the solidarity between living and dead warriors, may also have been expressed in murals depicting vultures attacking headless men. The absence of a head was apparently a stylistic convention in Çatal paintings, indicating death, real or initiatory. The vulture is believed to have been an agent for removing the flesh from the bones of the dead before they were buried

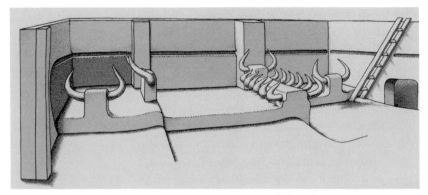

Fig. 35 Single "bull pillars" and "bull bench" from east end of Çatal Höyük VI.61 (after Mellaart, 1963)

beneath the platforms in the Çatal chambers. The fact that the vulture at figure 36 was given human legs sends us again to Bruce Lincoln, who writes that Indo-Iranian warrior initiations often involved the facing-down of a mock "monster," a realistic dummy of a feared beast. If this kind of initiation was in fact practiced at Çatal Höyük, the human legs protruding from vulture images here and in other Çatal murals suggest a rite in which men dressed as vultures enacted the ritual death of the novice. The skull shown beneath the bull's head would again most likely have been that of a deceased warrior, Lincoln's "celestial counterpart" of the living warrior-initiate.[126]

The Fire at Çatal VI

Çatal Höyük was occupied for approximately a thousand years, from c. 7300 BC to c. 6300 BC. Midway in the seventh millennium, the settlement at Level VI was destroyed by fire, a conflagration so intense that all bacterial decay was arrested, leaving perishable items like wooden containers (fig. 32) and fine woven cloth in an exceptional state of preservation. Among the ruins of the fire, excavators also found an intriguing collection of stone statuettes, two of which are reproduced above (fig. 33). These apparently long-held and handed-down figurines, many of which showed the mending of ancient breaks, stand in marked contrast to the wall constructions, which, by the time of the fire, had become distinctly overblown and ill-maintained.

Before Level VI, no structure at Çatal Höyük had been burned; each had stood until it became uninhabitable before being rebuilt. Mellaart found that up to 120 layers of plaster had accumulated on the chamber walls in the previous levels (VIII and VII), causing them to lean precariously under the weight.[144] The condition of the vulture-bull chamber at figure 36 was described as "appalling," with every wall near collapse and the platform around the hearth littered with animal bones.[143] Burials in various chambers had apparently become so numerous that they could no longer be contained in their usual resting place under the platforms, and some had spilled out into the space beneath the floors of these rooms. Mellaart also noted that less care seems to have been taken to leave earlier burials undisturbed;[145] bones and skulls were found rearranged and funeral gifts scattered, mirroring the carelessness observed *page 23* at late PPNB sites elsewhere.

The structures at Level VI had acquired almost 200 layers of plaster when the entire settlement was destroyed by the intense fire mentioned above. When a much smaller settlement was built over the

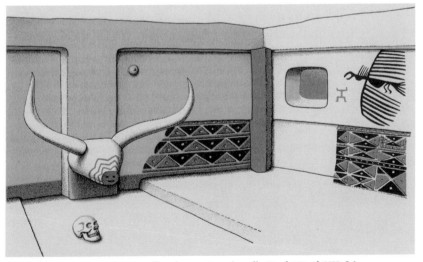

Fig. 36 Reconstruction of west wall and part of north wall, Çatal Höyük VII.21 (after Mellaart, 1967)

ruins, excavators found the mood of the site significantly changed. The monumental wall constructions were no longer erected, nor were the multiple-horned bull benches, although single bull pillars still appeared occasionally. The ceremonial flint knives were gone, and while obsidian weapons continued to be made, their size and number decreased until, by Level II, the industry was distinctly impoverished. With only a single human skull reported in these upper strata (at Level V), one assumes that this form of ancestor worship, characteristic of PPNB culture for more than two thousand years, was diminished as well.

Little is known of the topmost levels at Çatal Höyük, which are badly eroded. For unknown reasons the settlement was then abandoned for a new location across the river. "Çatal Höyük West" has not yet been excavated, but soundings show that geometrically painted pottery was present in the lowest levels of the new site, as it had been from Level III of the old settlement.[147]

In studying the figurines recovered from the original site, Mary Voigt found evidence of what she called "a shift in religious practice" after Level VI at Çatal Höyük. Stone figurines like those at figures 33 and 34 were no longer crafted, and Voigt believes that a group of these (largely male) figurines had been intentionally entombed at Level VI, perhaps an indication that the images had lost power.[224] In the later (largely female) statuette collection from upper levels (V-II) at Çatal Höyük, themes associated with birth, renewal, and abundance seem to be dominant.

The dating of the strata at Çatal Höyük is controversial. Mellaart placed the conflagration at Level VI at c. 6500 BC[147], but the present excavator, Ian Hodder, believes it should be dated earlier.[101] If the great fire did occur c. 6500 BC, or later, it would be tempting to see the subsequent disintegration of the Vedic-like traditions at Çatal Höyük as what happened when Zarathustra's reforms reached an ancient stronghold of Indo-European culture. As noted earlier, the immense number of actual horn cores of bulls used in the wall constructions before the fire at Level VI could well have been indicative of the excesses of cattle sacrifice that Zarathustra denounced in the *Gathas*.

page 90

If, on the other hand, the destruction of Level VI is to be dated before 6500 BC, the fire and the subsequent dying-out of former traditions might instead have been caused by raiders who, in taking the cattle of Çatal Höyük, stole the spiritual as well as the economic wealth of this old site. In any case, the change in religious orientation after Level VI, followed by the appearance of geometrically painted ceramics, argues for the arrival here of the same influence that inspired the founding of painted pottery communities across the Middle East and southeast Europe.

That this influence may not have been entirely welcome in the region is suggested by the volatile situation here and elsewhere in Turkey during this period. Mellaart noted with curiosity that while no building below Çatal VI had been destroyed by fire, every settlement level thereafter (V-II) was burned.[144] On the coast, the settlement at Mersin was also destroyed by fire, soon after the appearance of the first clearly Halaf ceramic motifs. Inland, the community at Çan Hasan was burned as well, again not long after the advent there of painted pottery. And to the west the settlement at Hacilar, whose fine painted pottery showed distinct influences from the east (fig. 37), was destroyed by fire several times in the first half of the sixth millennium before finally being abandoned for good.[147]

Fig. 37
Painted pottery from
Hacilar, southwest Turkey
(after Mellaart, 1970)

These events appear to have been more or less contemporary with the demise of the relocated site of Çatal Höyük West after it too suffered what may have been destruction by fire.[146] In contrast to the remarkable developments taking place in lands to the east and west, the ensuing period in Turkey has been described as one of "retrogression."[147] If those who introduced painted pottery into late seventh and sixth millennium settlements in Turkey were in fact followers of Zarathustra, these several site destructions could indicate the presence there of others who were resistant to the way of the prophet.

Returning to the earlier settlement at Çatal Höyük, it is from that site and the surrounding region that Colin Renfrew sees early forms of Indo-European language spreading west, accompanying the first farmers of Europe.[183] Others have theorized a migration of Çatal traditions eastward into northern Iraq, where Halafian pottery designs show distinct similarities to the iconography of Çatal Höyük.[74] It is certainly possible that more than one Indo-European dialect was represented at this huge settlement before its demise, and if so, the breaking up of Çatal traditions might coincide with the diffusion of Indo-European-speaking peoples to the east as well as the west, a possibility that will be explored in the next chapter.

CHAPTER EIGHT

The Indo-European Framework:
A Brief Excursus

"That the [Indo-European] homeland has been discovered,
there can be no doubt, as it has been sought everywhere from
the North to the South poles and from the Atlantic to the
Pacific. Temporally, it has been located anywhere between
80,000 BC (Neanderthals) and c. 1600 BC (the expansion of
chariot warfare from eastern Anatolia)."

— James P. Mallory,
"The Homelands of the Indo-Europeans"

It would be impossible to review here all of the theories that have been
proposed for the homeland and dispersal of the Indo-European family
of languages. No hypothesis has found lasting consensus, and scholars
disagree on even the most basic aspects of the problem. As one observer
describes the present impasse: "Typically a convincing and detailed
proposal offered in one field (e.g., archaeology) is undermined by
evidence from another (i.e., linguistics) and vice versa."[33]

Surveying the confusion surrounding this question, one eminent
authority has urged those working on the location of the Iranian
homeland in particular to frame their theories within the context of a
comprehensive solution of the Indo-European problem as a whole.[134]
I have no formal training in the science of linguistics, but as we do
intend to explore the question of the Iranian homeland — in light of
the possibility that Zarathustra lived in the seventh millennium — I can
at least honor that request by placing our investigation within an Indo-
European framework.

As noted earlier, the Indo-European family includes not only the languages of Europe (with the exception of Finnish, Basque, and Hungarian) but those historically associated with Iran and India as well. All of these languages are presumed to have emanated from a single "proto-Indo-European" ancestor—or a cluster of closely related Indo-European dialects[245]—that splintered and dispersed at an unknown time in prehistory. It is important to keep in mind, however, that no proto-Indo-European text is known to exist; the material culture and physical remains of proto-Indo-Europeans cannot be identified without intense controversy; and the geographical location of their homeland has been the subject of "a century and a half of intense yet inconclusive debate."[133]

At the present time there are two prominent theories regarding Indo-European origins, each of which has apparent weaknesses. One theory holds that the proto-Indo-Europeans were nomadic horsemen-pastoralists living in the steppes north of the Black Sea in the fourth millennium BC. The domestication of the horse and the invention of the wheel supposedly enabled these "Kurgan" peoples to conquer territories to the west, thus bringing Indo-European languages into Europe.[80, 81] Critics of this theory argue that Indo-European languages are so different from one another that they are likely to have begun separating before 4000 BC. The ability of pastoralists from the steppes to impose their language on so much of Bronze Age Europe has been called into question as well.[55]

page 93 The other theory, originally formulated by Colin Renfrew and mentioned here earlier, identifies Neolithic settlers of Turkey as the proto-Indo-Europeans, who in the seventh millennium carried their language, along with the agricultural way of life, west into Greece (and eventually to Iran and the Indus Valley by way of the Central Asian steppes).[183, 184] The main objection to this view seems to involve the time depth. According to one critic: "Given the tendency of geographically dispersed languages to drift apart from their common prototype, it is by no means certain that after 8,000 years the languages introduced by the first farmers in Europe could even be recognized as having had a common origin."[203b] But the defenders of this theory note that there is in fact no solid set of criteria to determine how well certain languages could have been conserved over extended periods of time. Not only are different languages known to have changed at different rates, but, as an Avestan scholar points out, religious or priestly language tends to be particularly slow to change, since religions are by nature conservative.[130]

The difficulty in establishing one or the other of these theories was made emphatically clear by the two authors of a recent publication on the subject, who admitted that they themselves hold differing views on which model is most viable.[55]

From our own perspective, the second theory would obviously be more congenial to the idea of an Indo-European-speaking prophet living in c. 6500 BC. Moreover, if we leave aside for the moment the question of time depth, many of the objections to the second theory could actually be resolved by the introduction of a charismatic religious figure with an agricultural bias into the seventh millennium milieu. For one thing, Renfrew's characterization of the people who migrated west to Greece as peaceful groups of Indo-European-speaking farmers has been faulted by some critics on the grounds that such an image contradicts the "heroic" warrior values of nomadic pastoralists like those in the *Rigveda*, values that many believe to be typical of early Indo-European culture.[81] But the proto-Indo-European economy was certainly not limited to herding, and comparative linguists have observed, on the basis of shared, well-developed, agricultural terminology, that proto-Indo-Europeans were also sedentary farmers.[8, 33]

As we have observed earlier, PPNB peoples were not only the original domesticators of herd animals, but, like the linguists' proto-Indo-Europeans, they were also sedentary and agricultural. Moreover, the archaeological record of the seventh millennium suggests that by 6500 BC, the PPNB weapons tradition was conserved in part by nomadic pastoralists whose crafting of arrow and spear heads is said to have retained "a cohesion with the whole of the previous PPNB."[37] These *page 24* well-armed herders might have continued to maintain the heroic-warrior tradition associated with the Indo-European pastoralists of the *Rigveda*, while the farmers who established agricultural settlements with painted pottery after 6500 BC represented the beginning of an Indo-European tradition in which the peaceful cultivation of the earth was more highly valued.

The seemingly contradictory images of Indo-Europeans — heroic warriors *and* peaceful farmers — could also be due to the existence of more than one stage in the dispersal and development of the Indo-European family of languages. According to one analyst, any model of early migrations must take into account "the stratification in depth of the Indo-European languages themselves."[69] It has been suggested that at least two waves of Indo-Europeans migrated into Greece, at two different times, an idea that would embrace both theories outlined above. The warlike Indo-Europeans from lands north of the Black Sea who began invading eastern Europe in the fourth millennium (the Kurgan culture of the first theory) would then have found descendants of at least one earlier wave already in place (Renfrew's seventh millennium Indo-European farmers). Other scholars agree that the dispersal of Indo-European languages through Europe was "not a uniform and continuous process, but a punctuated, multi-stage and repetitive one."[245]

If this is true for Europe, might the dispersal of Indo-European languages into Iran and India have been accomplished in several stages as well? Ancestors of the Indian and Iranian peoples are conventionally placed in the fourth-millennium steppes of southern Russia, either as indigenous peoples or migrating pastoralists who had moved into the steppes after the theorized seventh millennium split of the Indo-European unity in Turkey (second theory, above). In these models, the appearance of "Grey Ware" in northern Iran in the first half of the third millennium BC usually marks the initial descent into Iran of the steppe-dwelling Indo-Iranians, who then separated from one another, as the theory goes, with the Indic branch moving off to the east through Afghanistan into northwest India.[74]

The appearance of Grey Ware in Iranian sites could indeed mark a southward movement of Indo-Europeans from the steppes, but the critical question is whether Grey Ware marks the *first* appearance of Indo-Europeans in Iran. If the multi-stage model offered above for the dispersal of the Indo-European languages of Europe can also be applied to the prehistory of Iran and India, the incoming Grey Ware people — like the fourth millennium incursion of Kurgan tribes into eastern Europe — may have encountered descendants of an earlier wave of Indo-Europeans among the various peoples inhabiting the Iranian plateau.

The Indo-European Wheel

Another objection to placing the proto-Indo-Europeans in the seventh millennium has centered around the several terms for "wheel" that appear to be held in common by all Indo-European languages, implying that the wheel was known to the Indo-European unity before, or soon after, it began breaking up. The earliest archaeological evidence of wheeled vehicles is dated to the fourth millennium BC, leading some prehistorians to assume that the wheel was not invented until that time, and that the dispersal of the Indo-European languages must therefore have occurred after 4000 BC. Further, the presence in the Avesta of the term *rathesta* (from the Iranian root word *ratha*, "wheel"), translated as "one standing on a chariot," has been interpreted to mean that Zarathustra himself could not have lived before the invention of the wheeled chariot early in the second millennium BC.[28]

But we know that the meaning of a word is likely to change over time,[49] and a survey of "wheel" words in other Indo-European languages reveals meanings that are often more symbolic than literal. For example, while the word for "wheel" in Avestan and Sanskrit is *ratha*, the related Latin word *rota* actually means "circle" as well as "wheel," and the alternative translations of the Germanic *rotho* (wheel) as "sun" or "sky" takes the meaning of this root word directly into the metaphorical.[74]

We earlier ventured an interpretation of the "wheeled-cross" patterns on the pottery of the late seventh millennium, suggesting that *page 75* this image may have been symbolic of the perfect world created by Ahura Mazda, when the sun stood still in the sky, directly overhead as at high noon. We then compared this symbol of static perfection with the so-called whirl patterns of the same period, patterns that seem to be "rotating" and are therefore possibly symbolic of the setting-into-motion of the sun that marked the beginning of time in the Zoroastrian tradition. As we saw in the map at figure 29, both of these symbolic kinds of "wheels" appeared on painted pottery from Greece to the Iranian plateau, lands in which Indo-European languages were spoken in historical times. Might we then ask if the shared Indo-European terms for "wheel" could have originated in the shared pottery symbols of the seventh and sixth millennia BC?

The Scope of Iranian Influence

One final point of interest concerns the wide influence that the Iranian language in particular seems to have enjoyed in other lands, even before the days of the Persian Empire. The similarity of linguistic features in Greek and Indo-Iranian languages has long been acknowledged, and recent research has demonstrated that it is actually the Iranian, rather than the Indian, language that most closely resembles Greek.[33] To explain this distinction, one scholar has suggested that the Indic and Iranian languages, which at one time had experienced a period of extensive contact within the larger Indo-European linguistic community, then suffered "a process of fragmentation" that resulted in the splitting off of Indic while Iranian was undergoing a series of shared innovations with the European languages.[123] This evaluation is not time-specific, and from the perspective taken here, the breaking away of Indic speakers from Iranian would most likely have begun when those PPNB peoples who refused Zarathustra's reforms chose instead to live — or continue living — nomadic ways of life.

The singular influence of the Iranian language was apparently felt by peoples outside the Indo-European family as well. Gamkrelidze and Ivanov have identified numerous lexical borrowings in Finno-Ugric languages that are "specifically early Iranian."* Again we have no knowledge of when those borrowings might have taken place, but these linguists tell us that the loan words show phonological features that are characteristic of the Iranian language immediately after its split from the Indo-Iranian dialect community. Notable among these early Iranian loanwords are terms used in agriculture, stockbreeding, and various crafts.[74]

It has further been suggested that these contacts with northern peoples were made by Iranian speakers who traveled up the east side of the Caspian Sea.[74] If these travelers were bearing Zarathustra's message, the archaeology of Transcaucasia suggests that these Iranian speakers

---

Finno-Ugric is a Uralic, rather than Indo-European, language family that includes Finnish and Hungarian.

might also have taken the *western* route around the Caspian to reach northern lands. The first farming settlements in the Kur and Araxes valleys, which lie west of the Caspian Sea in Transcaucasia, were founded early in the sixth millennium, and the similarity of their round houses to the rounded Halafian "tholoi" has suggested to some observers that Halaf was the probable influence behind the shift to agriculture in the Caucasus.[147]

We earlier noted that Halafian pottery, decorated with symbols that seem particularly expressive of Zarathustra's teachings, spread far *page 76* beyond the parameters of the culture itself. The origin of the Halaf tradition is unknown, but certain aspects of this culture have encouraged analysts to compare it with some of the traditions of Çatal Höyük.[30] Gamkrelidze and Ivanov have suggested that Halaf was in fact an Indo-European culture that evolved from the migration of former occupants of Çatal Höyük eastward into northern Iraq.[74] As noted earlier, Halafian sites did yield occasional arrowheads and human skulls, but in contrast to the actual bulls' horns used in numerous Çatal constructions (figs. 35, 36), the bucrania of Halaf were restricted to motifs on stylized pottery and amulets (figs. 22a, 25). Furthermore, the round, free-standing Halafian "tholoi" (fig. 26) bore no resemblance to the agglutinative and strictly rectangular Çatal architecture (fig. 1).

Together with indications that Halaf surfaced several hundred years after the earliest of the painted pottery cultures, these various observations suggest that if the Halafians had previously been members of the same Indo-European tradition (or traditions) that informed Çatal Höyük, they may have lived as nomads for some time before being converted to the way of Zarathustra. The late emergence of Halaf would then represent a well-documented example of the ongoing success of missionary efforts, perhaps emanating from Iran, among the indigenous nomadic peoples of northern Iraq.

If such was indeed the case, the excellence and individuality of Halafian ceramics would demonstrate the extraordinary creativity that was released from the peaceful fusion of former traditions with the word of the prophet. The subsequent expansion of Halaf culture and influence suggests that, once converted, the Halafians became remarkably adept at spreading the teachings of Zarathustra across the Near East, contacting both Indo-European and non-Indo-European peoples, perhaps reinforcing the prophet's ideas among settled communities while persuading the unconverted to follow the way of *asha*. If this picture is correct, the *page 51* disappearance of Halaf in the fifth millennium is likely to have marked the diminishing, if not the end, of Zarathustra's influence in lands west of Iran.

CHAPTER NINE

Zarathustra's Homeland and His Place of Refuge

"The study of the history of Zoroastrianism is a discipline involving great efforts of speculation and imagination."

— Albert de Jong,
*Traditions of the Magi: Zoroastrianism
in Greek and Latin Literature*

If we have established a plausible congruence between the archaeology of the seventh millennium and the traditions surrounding Zarathustra, can we now reverse the direction of our inquiry? Having invoked his presence to explain the massive spread of agriculture after 6500 BC, it may now be possible to use the archaeology of that time to clarify and expand our knowledge of Zarathustra's own life and activities, including, perhaps, his elusive homeland. To this end I would encourage the reader, now possessed of the basic facts pertaining to our investigation, to participate in the processes of speculation and imagination that historians of Zoroastrianism — and the most generative archaeologists — have found essential in building their theories.

The conflicting claims regarding the birthplace of the prophet *page 57* were noted earlier. Some scholars argue that he came from the west, citing ancient Persian traditions that situate the native home of Zarathustra near Lake Urmia in northwest Iran.[241,108,48] Others maintain that the recognizable place-names in the Younger Avesta point to a homeland in eastern Iran, which in antiquity extended into what is today Afghanistan.[28, 130] Their differences are sometimes reconciled by theorizing that Zarathustra was born in one of these regions and later lived and worked in the other.[161] And since one of the most enduring Zoroastrian traditions tells of the prophet leaving his original home to seek refuge elsewhere, his birthplace and his ultimate center of activity may well lie at some distance from one another.

page 58

First the question of his birthplace, his homeland. Since the possible existence of more than one historical Zarathustra could be affecting the dispute over whether his home was in eastern or western Iran, we should specifically be asking which of the two regions is most likely to have been the birthplace of the prophet *in the seventh millennium BC*. Although scholars disagree about whether his people were nomads or settlers, Mary Boyce believes that Zarathustra's expressed desire in the *Gathas* for peace "in the dwelt-in abodes" (Y. 53.8) refers to permanent settlements[28] — distinctly good news for the archaeological investigator. We would then be looking for a settled community (or a particular culture to which such a community might belong) in either eastern or western Iran that was already in existence before c. 6500 BC and was related in some way to the late PPNB tradition from which, according to our theory, Zarathustra broke away.

page 81

From an archaeological point of view, the concentration of PPNB culture in lands west of Iran (see map at fig. 5) might favor placing the prophet's homeland in the west. But the geographical sweep of PPNB influence that is now coming to light suggests that settlements related to that culture may have been present in the east as well. For example, it had long been presumed that agriculture was unknown in Pakistan and India before the fourth millennium BC, but recent excavations in Baluchistan (northwest Pakistan) have uncovered domesticated plants and animals in the lowest levels of the settlement at Mehrgarh, dating to perhaps the eighth or early seventh millennium.[110] These were the same species known to western sites, and the added presence of rectangular architecture, polished greenstone axes, and in the early levels a complete absence of pottery further links this eastern settlement to the PPNB tradition that dominated the west in this period.[202]

page 22

Mehrgarh is also believed to be related to the two excavated tells at Sang-e Caxamaq in northeastern Iran (map at fig. 17). The older of these tells was apparently founded before the middle of the seventh millennium, and although incompletely excavated, it was aceramic and *page 22* contained rectangular houses whose floors often bore traces of the red-stained lime plaster associated with PPNB. This older community at Sang-e Caxamaq, together with the related village at Mehrgarh, would therefore offer a model of an eastern cultural tradition into which Zarathustra could have been born in the mid-seventh millennium BC.

The simple red-on-buff painted pottery that was present in base levels of the later settlement at Sang-e Caxamaq, estimated to c. 6300 *page 45* BC, was "distinguished by its conservatism," displaying a limited range of forms and geometric patterns.[196] Persian literary sources suggest that while the people of the region into which Zarathustra was born were initially resistant to his reforms, they were eventually converted to the faith. If his kinsmen nevertheless retained their conservative tendencies, the relative backwardness of the newer settlement at Sang-e Caxamaq and the connections of the older tell to PPNB traditions might further support the idea that eastern Iran was the homeland Zarathustra left behind.

On the other hand, the argument favoring a homeland in western Iran seems equally plausible from the perspective of seventh millennium archaeology. A variety of sources within Persian and Arabic literature claimed that the legendary hearth of the Iranian people lay in northwest Iran and that it was there, specifically around Lake Urmia, that Zarathustra was born.[28] We noted earlier that the first agricultural settlements in northwestern Iran — a handful of sites scattered around Lake Urmia and known to archaeologists as the Hajii Firuz culture — *page 40* were founded in the seventh millennium, with traces of red-stained floors within rectangular mud-brick houses suggesting ties to PPNB. Originally estimated to date from c. 6500 BC, the settlement of Hajii Firuz itself may actually be somewhat older, as its earliest pottery designs are said to be closely tied to the "proto-Hassuna" sites (see below) of northern Iraq.[225] Hajii Firuz pottery shows links to the Iranian plateau as well as to northern Iraq, but when compared to the dynamic activity in both of those regions during this period, the Hajii Firuz culture as a whole was deemed conservative by its excavator.[222]

Like Sang-e Caxamaq in the northeast, these northwestern sites around Lake Urmia seem too far outside the main stream of cultural change in this period to have been the center from which that change emanated. But again this conservatism could mean that northwest Iran was instead the homeland from which Zarathustra fled. In any case, the region around Lake Urmia figures prominently in Zoroastrian traditions and will be revisited in the next chapter when we explore the relationship of Zarathustra to the order of the Magi, historically a Zoroastrian priesthood of western Iran whose association with Lake Urmia was well known in the ancient world.

The Community of Refuge

As for Zarathustra's place of refuge, the Avesta gives no indication of how far the prophet might have traveled before he was taken in page 58 by "Vishtaspa," his lifelong patron. The distances now known to have been covered by Neolithic and even earlier peoples place few theoretical restrictions on the length of that journey. From as early as 12,000 BC, obsidian from eastern Turkey was reaching sites in the Zagros mountains that lie more than 500 miles from the obsidian source.[118] And in the seventh millennium, the turquoise discovered in southwest Iranian settlements is believed to have been obtained from deposits 400 miles to the northeast.[147] One archaeologist pointed out that such items may have been handled through intermediate trading stations, but he felt that it was also likely that some individuals traveled the entire distances.[135] In short, as another prehistorian observed, "We now accept that neither mountains nor seas were ever barriers to communication or to the movement of materials and peoples."[141] There is thus no reason to limit the range of Zarathustra's initial journey — or the distances traveled by those who would later carry his word to other lands.

With few spatial restrictions, our search for Zarathustra's community of refuge must primarily be governed by the element of time. That is, the earliest and most lasting of the new painted pottery settlements would seem to be the most likely candidates for the community that became his sanctuary and center of activity. If, for example, the prophet had been born in the region around Lake Urmia and traveled south seeking refuge, he would soon have found himself in the vicinity of what would become the oldest of the fine painted pottery traditions of Iraq, the Hassuna culture of c. 6500 BC. Not far from the site of *page 40* Hassuna itself, several small hamlets with archaic pottery (Tell Sotto, Kultepe) provide evidence of a settled population which prehistorians believe slightly predates and anticipates the Hassuna culture.[10] But these "proto-Hassuna" sites were small and relatively short-lived, while Zarathustra's religious base would surely have remained a vital center long after his death. Of the Hassuna settlements themselves, perhaps only the famous and enduring site of Nineveh, about which little is known in this early period, would theoretically fit the model.

Looking east, the Iranian plateau may hold more promise as the location of Zarathustra's community of refuge, particularly in light of the lasting impact of the Sialk/Cheshmeh Ali plateau culture on *page 47* virtually all of Iran. In antiquity, Iran's main trade route ran through the north-central plateau, linking the ancient city of Raga to central Asia on the east and to northern Iraq and the valleys of the Tigris and Euphrates on the west.[28] According to one authority: "No doubt this route or one much like it, which follows river courses and traverses mountain ranges at obvious passes, was already travelled in prehistoric times."[179] If Zarathustra had followed this natural route in the seventh millennium BC, he could easily have reached sites on the northern plateau from either eastern or western Iran, i.e., from either of the regions that have been theorized as the place of his birth.

As noted earlier, archaeological information from the Iranian plateau is extremely scarce for this period; both Sialk and Cheshmeh Ali were investigated before modern technology could make the most *page 44* of what was there. But even without precise archaeological data, the importance of the north-central plateau in Iranian history suggests that it played a major part in that country's prehistory as well.* The excavations at Sialk, however limited, show it to have been an important settlement from the earliest times. The miniature mortars and pestles that were elsewhere made in stone were fashioned in pottery as well

---

Even in the time of the Persian Empire (550–330 BC), when the southern province of Fars was home to the Achaemenian dynasty, topography and the natural lines of communication dictated that the vital center of Iran lay on the northern plateau.[28]

as stone at Sialk, and while bone sickle hafts were found at several Iranian sites, none was as fine as the carved bone knife handle with its unexpectedly Persian-like figure recovered from Sialk 1 (fig. 27).

page 72

But it is the settlement at Cheshmeh Ali whose painted pottery has been described by one analyst as "decidedly more mature" than elsewhere on the plateau.[131] And another authority, acknowledging the high quality of cultural forms at the related site of Sialk, concluded that those at Cheshmeh Ali were nevertheless superior: "If the presence of a more highly developed repertoire of designs and ceramic forms may be interpreted as meaning that a site is close to the focus of a culture, we could consider that Cheshmeh Ali is nearer the center of this culture than Sialk."[140]

We have already observed that the mound of Cheshmeh Ali lies immediately adjacent to the ruins of the ancient plateau city of Raga, which played such a significant role in Zoroastrian history. The tentative

page 81

identification of Raga as the "Ragha" mentioned in the Younger Avesta may be supported by the fact that Raga was historically one of the holiest places of the Median Magi. The members of this western Zoroastrian priesthood are said to have looked upon Raga as "the original center of the faith — their Rome, as it were, or Canterbury."[28] Raga remained an important center of Zoroastrianism into early Islamic times, known for its famous shrine of Zoroastrian origin as well as "Iran's purest spring."[131] If the nearby site of Cheshmeh Ali was not Zarathustra's primary religious base in the seventh millennium, the richness of its ceramic tradition, its lasting effect on Iranian culture, and its close proximity to ancient Raga suggest that Cheshmeh Ali played a critical role in the development of his vision.

Continuing this line of reasoning, if Zarathustra's center of activity was on the north-central plateau, some of his earliest disciples would theoretically have traveled west, influencing those who founded the Hassuna and Samarra painted pottery cultures of mid-to-late seventh millennium Iraq. We have observed the similarities between the early

page 45

(Sialk-style) ceramics of the plateau and those of Hassuna-Samarra. A few centuries later, links between northern Iraq and the Iranian plateau had become even more evident through the remarkable pottery styles of Halaf and Cheshmeh Ali. As one analyst observed, the painted pottery of Halaf reveals "a range of designs of which the essentials are also to be found on the Iranian plateau."[106] Was this connection to the plateau actually responsible for the emergence of Halaf? As suggested in the last chapter, the transformation of an indigenous nomadic people of *page 107* northern Iraq into the immensely successful Halafian culture may have been one of the most enduring accomplishments of missionaries from the Iranian plateau.

The Halaf tradition continued to grow and expand its influence for more than a thousand years, until it was replaced by the pre-Sumerian 'Ubaid culture of the southern delta, which spread into northern Iraq in *page 51* the fifth millennium BC. The ultimate fate of the Halafians themselves is unknown, but according to one prehistorian, while 'Ubaid was moving into northern Iraq, "all of Iran was affected in varying degrees by Halaf culture."[140] If this is true, the further enrichment of Iranian plateau pottery at this time with motifs associated with Halaf may mean that with the coming of 'Ubaid, the Halafians retreated east to the sanctuary of like believers in centers on the Iranian plateau. As we will see in the next chapter, the painted pottery tradition as a whole endured longer in Iran than in Iraq. And by the time the Zoroastrian religion entered history, what was once to have been a faith for all mankind was identified with the Iranian people alone.[27]

CHAPTER TEN

Entering History:
the Median Magi, the Persian Empire,
and the Muslim Invasion

"The prehistoric civilization is of supreme importance in Iran. The red-ware [Sialk/Cheshmeh Ali] culture, the oldest on the plateau, displays features which will continue without interruption: it is at the source of the country's artistic tradition."

— Yolanda Maleki, "Abstract Art and Animal Motifs Among the Ceramics of the Region of Tehran"

For more than three thousand years, the enduring tradition of painted pottery that began in the last half of the seventh millennium was the principle artistic expression of the village communities of Iran.[216] In the west, painted ceramics became increasingly schematic and cursive until they finally disappeared, but the tradition persisted in eastern Iran until the middle of the third millennium BC. Even after the emergence of urban civilizations in southern Iraq and adjacent southwestern Iran, the tradition of painted pottery continued to be faithfully maintained in east Iranian villages.[213] If these patterned ceramics did in fact reflect the teachings of Zarathustra, the persistence of painted pottery in eastern Iran suggests that those teachings may also have been conserved in that region, a possibility that would be supported by the presence of east *page 109* Iranian place-names in the Younger Avesta.

The lay of Iranian land might also have contributed to the endurance of this tradition. Throughout Iran's history, the plains are known to have been the melting-pots of various peoples, while the mountains provided secluded areas where religious beliefs, traditions, and customs could be maintained in relative isolation from the sweep of historical events. According to one observer, "the surprising survival of motifs and techniques in Iranian art over many centuries, and even millennia, may be explained by the traditions maintained in these refuge areas." [179] If, after pottery was no longer painted with symbolic motifs, the ideology expressed in those symbols was maintained in the oral tradition of one or more of these isolated areas, the teachings of Zarathustra could have been preserved in eastern Iran until Zoroastrianism emerged as the religion of the Persian Empire.

The Order of the Magi

Fragments of Zarathustra's vision may have survived in the west as well. Before it was incorporated into the Persian Empire, the kingdom of the Medes (Media) extended from the Iranian plateau to beyond the Tigris (map at fig. 38). According to Herodotus (I.101), the Medes themselves were composed of six tribes, one of which, the "magoi" (better known by the plural, "magi," of the Latin singular, "magus"), was a hereditary priesthood, passing exclusively from father to son. In the days of the Persian Empire, the Magi served as advisors to the Achaemenian kings, claiming the teachings of Zarathustra as their special province. According to one scholar: "From the earliest references to the religion of the Persians to the latest sources taken into account, the Magi were the supreme symbol of the religious life of the Zoroastrians." [49]

Learned Greeks and Romans of antiquity claimed that the order of the Magi was founded by Zarathustra himself and charged with transmitting his teachings. We have noted Plutarch's reference to Zarathustra as "the Magian." Dio Chrysostom wrote in his *Oratorio* (36.41) that Zarathustra established the religion of the Magi, while in the *Menippus* (6-8) Lucian described the Magi as "the disciples and successors of Zoroaster." As summarized by the classical scholar, Albert de Jong: "That Zoroaster was perceived to be the first of the Magi is a common enough tradition, and — in view of the claim of the Zoroastrian priesthood that the entire Avesta derives from Zoroaster — substantially correct." [49]

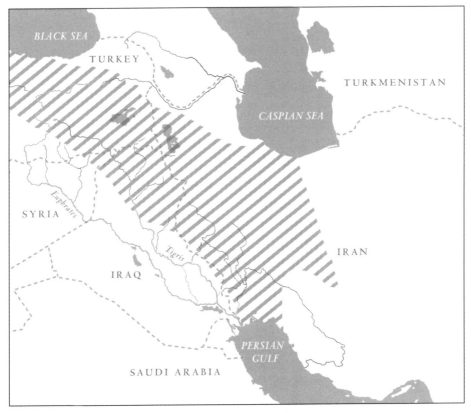

Fig. 38 Media, the kingdom of the Medes, in the first millennium BC

But could a seventh millennium Zarathustra have been the first of the Magi? Or, phrased differently, could some form of the hereditary order of the Magi date back to Neolithic times? As we saw earlier, the Zarathustra that Plutarch referred to as "the Magian" is the same individual that Plutarch placed 5,000 years before the siege of Troy.[178] And the passage from Xanthus's *Lydian History* entitled "On the Magi," was recounted as follows: "Xanthus the Lydian says that six thousand years passed from the time of Zoroaster up to the crossing of Xerxes, and that after him there have been many Magi in succession."[57] In his *Letters* (58.31), the Roman philosopher Seneca recorded the presence of Magi in Athens at the time of Plato's death, honoring him as an extraordinary individual, and it has been suggested that at that time

page 54

they provided Eudoxus and Aristotle with the dating of Zarathustra to 6,000 years before the death of Plato.[114] Albert de Jong has noted the emphasis placed upon the continuous succession of the members of this hereditary priesthood.[49] But again, could the Magian lineage have remained intact for 6,000 years?

Once more, the time span we are considering is immense, but what is known of the history of the Magi is so often confused and even contradictory that one suspects that their order endured many cycles of decay and rejuvenation before its name appeared in written records of the first millennium BC. For Christians, the Magi have always been identified with the "wise men from the east" who, in the gospel of Matthew and later commentaries, were guided by a star to the birth at Bethlehem. But modern scholars find the Magi to be among the most challenging enigmas of the ancient world, "associated with the highest speculation and the most base charlatanism; the mixed resources of religion and magic; a mysterious origin and an authority that endures across the succession of beliefs."[22]

Portrayed as sorcerers in popular fable, the Magi were recognized by the more serious Greeks and Romans (Dio Chrysostom, Apuleius) as dedicated servants of the gods. They were known throughout the ancient world for possessing strange and unfathomable powers; their name itself has come down to us in the discredited phenomenon we call magic. But in the *Greater Alcibiades* (I.122A), a commentary attributed to Plato distinguishes between two kinds of magic: popular magic, which is denigrated as sorcery, and authentic or "Persian magic," which is considered to be a form of religion, "the worship of the gods."

The relationship of the Magi to Zarathustra is no less controversial. They have been regarded on the one hand as an aboriginal tribe of necromancers and sorcerers who were responsible for the degradation of Zoroastrianism, and on the other as Zarathustra's true disciples and his missionaries in western Iran.[66] If the Magi — and Zarathustra — do in fact date back to the seventh millennium, both of these descriptions may have been accurate at one time or another over the ensuing epochs. And again the possibility of more than one "Zarathustra," with more than one kind of relationship to the Magi, should not be overlooked.

page 81

Seventh Millennium Masters of Fire?

The ancient historians' claim that the order of the Magi dates, like its founder, to the seventh millennium BC may be further supported by the remarkable technological achievements among the painted pottery communities of that period. According to the religious historian Mircea Eliade, a part of Zarathustra's originality was his emphasis on "the religious value of wisdom, that is, of science, of accurate and useful knowledge."[66] The natural sciences would have been particularly useful in an earth-centered religion that urged mankind to assist all elements of the Good Creation in achieving the perfection — the purity — of *page 62* their origins. In historical times the Magi were known not only for their allegiance to Zoroastrian principles but also for their mastery of the sacred element of fire. Their Neolithic counterparts, if such did exist, would surely have been interested in the effects of fire's transformative power on earthly substance.

Both the firing of clay and the smelting of metals enjoyed an extraordinary degree of development within the painted pottery cultures of Iran and Iraq. One ceramic analyst has suggested that in Neolithic times the creation of pottery was looked upon as a mystical or magical activity, that potters would have been seen as "the ones with power to transform matter through the control of fire."[221] In Karen Vitelli's view, knowing how to manipulate the element of fire would have invested certain Neolithic individuals with exceptional powers, a status accorded to early metallurgists as well as potters.[220] Given that many of the most important prehistoric advances in ceramics and metallurgy took place in lands that would later be associated with the Magi, is it possible that Vitelli's Neolithic masters of fire were ancestral — either figuratively or literally — to the members of this hereditary priesthood?

As noted earlier, the first Near Eastern pottery preceded the date *page 23* proposed here for Zarathustra by at least five hundred years. Therefore, if the prophet was indeed the first Magus, pottery was not a Magian invention. But we have also observed that after c. 6500 BC, the quality of the existing, rather primitive painted pottery of Iran and Iraq began to be enhanced, not only by an increasing complexity in shapes and geometric designs but also by a significant increase in firing temperatures, which produced a finer, harder ceramic with greater durability.

The means by which these higher temperatures were achieved was revealed at the Halafian site of Yarim Tepe II, where excavators recently uncovered two-stage pottery kilns dating to the sixth millennium BC, two thousand years before what formerly was the earliest known evidence of such advanced kilns. The combustion chambers at Yarim Tepe II were sunk into the ground, and each was roofed with a massive plate of clay pierced by some fifty apertures. Hot air was conducted through these openings into the domed upper stage where the pots were fired.[150] Capable of producing temperatures great enough to melt copper for casting, these kilns allowed Halafian potters to create strongly contrasted light-dark patterning on eggshell-thin ceramics whose technical excellence has yet to be surpassed.

page 49

In our earlier analysis of the ceramic designs themselves, we offered interpretations of the wheeled cross and whirl patterns based on the Zoroastrian creation myth, which is evoked in the *yasna* ceremony. We also noted the scholarly opinion that the richly patterned surfaces of the painted ceramics of this period represented an ideological heritage that was being transmitted across very large areas. Recalling that the later, historical Magi were both masters of fire and disseminators of Zarathustra's wisdom, one might logically expect to find their seventh-millennium counterparts engaged not only in the development of advanced firing techniques but also in the distribution of patterned ceramics carrying the teachings of the prophet.

page 75

page 74

This line of reasoning could also help to explain the idiosyncrasies of the well-documented Halafian "ceramic trade," which was conducted on a much larger scale than anything recorded before that time.[154] Neutron activation studies have shown that the fine ceramics of Halaf were actually produced in a limited number of centers and then circulated to outlying communities, without any reciprocal pottery being traded back into those centers. In the eyes of one observer, the stylistic unity of designs extending over the vast Halafian territory is thus even more remarkable: "The uniformity of Halaf motifs coupled with the circulation of pottery from specialized production sites implies that local elites were attempting to control the production not only of the pots but also of the important symbols—the metalinguistic code—that facilitated the exchange of goods over long distances and across many local ethnic boundaries."[239] Again, were these "local elites" ancestors of the historical Magi, overseeing the circulation of ceramics whose painted symbols reinforced the message of Zarathustra?

Neolithic ancestors of the Magi may also have utilized their mastery of fire to extract pure metal from ores. At one time, Zarathustra's use of the expression "molten metal" in the *Gathas* (Y. 32.7)* would have removed any possibility that he could have lived in the seventh millennium BC. (Although cold-hammered copper beads and other items were known from PPNB times, the actual smelting of copper was once thought to have been achieved no earlier than c. 4500 BC.) But recent excavations indicate that the smelting of both copper and lead actually date back at least as far as the beginning of the sixth millennium, and if the identification of copper slag at Level VI of Çatal Höyük holds true,[159] "molten metal" was known as early as c. 6500 BC.

Once more, some of the most notable discoveries in this realm have taken place within the well-excavated context of Halaf. As noted above, the two-stage pottery kilns discovered at Halafian Yarim Tepe II were capable of achieving temperatures hot enough for smelting, and various copper items (beads, pendants) were in fact recovered here and elsewhere in this period.[151] A little later, cast copper objects were produced at Halafian Arpachiyah,[136] while on the Iranian plateau a workshop for coppersmiths—complete with crucible, kiln, and molds—was in operation at Tepe Gabristan (map at fig. 17) in the sixth millennium BC.[129b]

The lead bracelet from Yarim Tepe was fashioned from exceptionally pure metal in which only trace amounts of silver could be identified.[151] And although copper was eventually used to make awls and other tools, the first metal objects appear to have been far from utilitarian, leaving prehistorians to wonder why metallurgy was pursued in the first place. A great deal of study will be needed to determine what

---

Some scholars believe this passage refers to an Iranian form of juridical ordeal-by-fire as well as to the molten metal that is expected to remove all vestiges of evil at the Zoroastrian end of time.[241]

the initial purpose of smelting might have been, but it seems fair to ask at this point if the extraction of metal from its ore might originally have been an effort, symbolic or real, to purify the mineral domain.

If some early form of the hereditary Magian priesthood was indeed responsible for the technological advances made within the painted pottery communities, those members associated with Halaf may have moved east to religious centers on the Iranian plateau when Halafian culture was replaced by 'Ubaid in northern Iraq. But it is also possible that they stayed put. What little we know of the historical Magi[22, 77] suggests that their prehistoric counterparts, or some of them, could have continued to function within the esoteric religious parameters of each of the succeeding cultures that ruled what is today northern Iraq and northwestern Iran, until the religion of Zarathustra came again to prominence in the land of the Medes.

page 115

Cyrus the Great

Cyrus II was a young prince of Fars (a province of southern Iran) who conquered all territory from the borders of India to Greece and established the Achaemenian dynasty (550-330 BC) to rule over this vast empire. Cyrus himself was apparently a practicing Zoroastrian and is credited with successfully holding together the Persian Empire by applying Zarathustra's principles of individual freedom of choice. As described by one scholar: "Instead of invoking fire, the sword, the mass deportation of whole populations, and the rigorous suppression of all nationalistic aspirations, he [Cyrus] conceded to the vanquished a high degree of cultural and political autonomy, including religious freedom. In other words, he accepted existing institutions and adapted himself to them; and he honoured the gods of all the people within his domain."[161] As mentioned earlier, a similar diversity—and a similar freedom—may have characterized the various painted pottery groups of the seventh and sixth millennia, some of whom might have chosen to retain their own religious traditions while at the same time responding to Zarathustra's agricultural imperative.

page 79

It has been suggested that Cyrus's allegiance to Ahura Mazda facilitated his conquest of not only eastern Iran, where the oldest known Zoroastrian communities were already established, but also the west, the land of the Medes. Mary Boyce has found indications that the "Ahuric doctrine" was already a dominant element in western Iran when Cyrus became king, so that "Zoroaster's teachings had the strength of embodying with what was new a number of already cherished beliefs and observances."[28] How the Ahuric doctrine found its way to western Iran before the establishment of the Persian Empire is unknown, but, as suggested above, some memory of Zarathustra's teachings might have been conserved by ancestors of the Magi who adapted their own esoteric traditions to the succession of cultures that later occupied northwest Iran and Iraq.* Or, as proposed for eastern Iran, the ancient doctrine might have been preserved in the isolated mountain refuges of northwestern Iran or the Caucasus, which many consider to have been the original homeland of the Median tribes.

After the Persian Empire

When written records begin to document the course of the Zoroastrian religion, its enduring resilience becomes clear. Even after the Persian empire was conquered by Alexander the Great and the Achaemenians replaced by the foreign dynasty of the Seleucids (305 BC), Zoroastrianism continued to thrive, not only in Iran but frequently in outlying regions — Syria, Palestine, Egypt — that were no longer under the rule of the Persians.[46] Mary Boyce finds the perseverance of these isolated communities to be a powerful testament to the inner strength of Zoroastrianism — and to the continuity created by the transmission of the faith "in the traditional way, that is, orally and by customary usage, from parent to child, without recourse to books."[28]

On the Iranian plateau, the holy city of Raga was refounded as a *page 114* Greek *polis* after the defeat of the Persian empire, but the town continued to be regarded as sacred. At this time, according to Boyce, the chief magus of Raga might have moved some of his priests, and the Zoroastrian

---

* *One of the last of these, the Assyrian Empire, made its capital at Nineveh, which was finally destroyed in 612 BC and never rebuilt.*

sacred fire, to what may have been considered the greater religious purity of Lake Urmia in northwestern Iran — the only part of the country that was still officially under Zoroastrian rule at the end of the fourth century BC. Boyce has further theorized that the claim in the *Bundahisn*, a late Persian collection of texts, that the region around Lake Urmia was

page 111 both the birthplace of Zarathustra and the homeland of the Iranians was a contrivance by these Magi to draw pilgrims away from Raga to their center at Urmia.[28] Whether or not her hypothesis is correct for events of the first millennium BC, it illustrates again the historical association of the Magi with both Lake Urmia and Raga — an association that may reach back to the late seventh millennium BC and the signs of contact

page 41 between the two regions that is revealed in the pottery of northwest Iran (the Hajii Firuz sites around Lake Urmia) and the Iranian plateau (Sialk, Cheshmeh Ali).

Zoroastrianism again became the state religion of Iran during the Parthian and Sasanian empires, which together lasted from the second century BC to the seventh century AD. The first Sasanian king took up the work of gathering and preserving the oral transmissions of the Avesta, inviting those who knew various passages by heart to recite them at court. Chosen works were then authorized to be part of the Sasanian Avesta and were learned and transmitted orally by Persian Magi for another two hundred years, until the priestly authorities finally allowed a written version to be prepared, using a specially invented alphabet that made it possible to record the Avestan sounds with some precision.[28]

In 642 AD the Sasanian empire was overthrown by the Muslim armies that swept out of Arabia, led by the second successor of Mohammed. Far more serious damage was done to the Zoroastrian tradition by the Arab invasion of Iran than by Alexander's conquest of the Persian Empire.[161] Religious persecutions, civil disruptions, and the burning of sacred texts by the Muslim conquerors forced many Zoroastrians to either give up their faith or go into exile. But a thousand years later, pockets of Zoroastrianism were still to be found within the borders of Iran. Europeans traveling through "Persia" in the seventeenth century AD reported encountering small, remote Zoroastrian communities whose survival under Islam was previously unknown in the West. The extent to which these European accounts agree with observations of the Persians recorded by Herodotus some two thousand years earlier (c. 450 BC) has again impressed modern scholars with the tenacity of Zarathustra's teachings.[28]

Included among these seventeenth century accounts are several that speak of the enduring devotion of the Zoroastrians to the ancient practices. One of the European travelers wrote that the Zoroastrians he met believed that the way to salvation was to work to purify the creations: "to till the ground, to cultivate the gardens, to keep the waters pure, to keep the fire alight." Another, a French merchant who was in Iran from 1665 to 1677, observed that agriculture was indeed the chief occupation of the Zoroastrians: "They regard it not only as a good and innocent calling but also as meritorious and noble, and they believe that it is the first of all vocations, that which the 'Sovereign God' and the 'Lesser Gods' [Ahura Mazda and the Amesha Spentas], as they say, approve of most and which they reward most amply. This opinion, made by them into an article of faith, causes them to turn naturally to work on the land."[29]

Today there are fewer than 150,000 Zoroastrians, most of whom live in India, where their ancestors fled during and after the Muslim invasion. Over time, and in the process of making their way in a new country, these "Parsis" of India shed some of the ancient beliefs and practices, but in remote Zoroastrian villages in Iran the old ways were faithfully conserved, "generation after hard-pressed generation," until the twentieth century AD.[28] In the 1970s, Iran's economic boom brought a new mobility to these isolated villagers, many of whom began migrating to industrial centers in Iran and elsewhere. As a result, most Zoroastrians today are city dwellers, with urban skills and a more secular worldview. But if the tenacious hold of the ancient religion has been loosened by contemporary urban culture, Zarathustra's teachings remain embedded in the foundations, both philosophical and economic, of modern civilization. His legacy forms the epilogue to our investigation.

CHAPTER ELEVEN

Epilogue:
The Legacy of Zarathustra

"My two earlier journeys to the East had led me to stumble many times across the traces of the Persian prophet and the religious ideas developed by his later followers. Often dismissed by pious Muslims as mere folklore, or falsely condemned as foreign influence, or even blankly denied even in the face of overwhelming evidence, the traces of Zarathustra's teachings refuse to fade away. In spite of everything, Zarathustra lives."

— Paul Kriwaczek, *In Search of Zarathustra*

In the course of his late twentieth century travels through Iran, Paul Kriwaczek, a British journalist, found traces of a deeper layer of religious tradition beneath the devotion to Islam: "an undercurrent of something else — hints and indications that behind the sincere dedication to the Qur'an there lay a hidden stratum of belief."[119] He concluded that thirteen hundred years of Islam — and, more recently, the modernizing of Iran — had failed to eradicate the spirit of Zarathustra. Fascinated by the endurance of this ancient religion, Kriwaczek began investigating the ways in which Zarathustra's teachings had influenced the belief systems of diverse peoples living at different periods of history, including our own. His book is a timely and original updating of questions that have intrigued western scholars since they first began translating the *Zend-Avesta* in the late nineteenth century, and discovering in the process an extraordinary similarity between Zoroastrianism and certain Judaic, Christian, and Islamic doctrines.

Over the ensuing decades of academic discourse, two main theories have emerged with regard to the original source of principles held in common by these religions, principles that range from ethical to theological and eschatological. One position claims that Zoroastrian ideas influenced Judaism and thence Christianity and Islam; the other maintains that it was the Jewish tradition that left its mark on Zoroastrianism. We know that the Jews came into close contact with the Zoroastrian religion when Cyrus conquered Babylon and released them from captivity in 539 BC, and some see this encounter as decisive in the subsequent development of Judaic thought.[161]

The possibility that similar religious ideas could have arisen independently within these faiths is also acknowledged among scholars, but as one observes, "it does not seem at all likely that so many similarities could have been formed in parallel independently." In spite of chronological difficulties in the documentation, he has concluded that "in most of the parallel points one may feel quite confident that the ideas were indigenous to Iran."[200]

Placing Zarathustra in the seventh millennium would undoubtedly establish the Iranian prophet as the first to voice several concepts that would later become — by whatever means — fundamental tenets of Judaism, Christianity, and Islam. We have mentioned the Zoroastrian belief in one supreme God, creator of the world, who is opposed by an evil power not within his control. Zoroastrians further believe that this evil power will *page 61n.* be annihilated at the end of time, when the perfection toward which the world is progressing will have been achieved. The realization of this goal is to be marked by the appearance of a cosmic saviour, the resurrection of the dead, final judgment, and the coming of the kingdom of God upon earth.[27] Although it has been suggested that the Zoroastrian eschatology was developed after the time of Zarathustra,[111] other Avestan scholars have found the seeds of all of these beliefs already present in the *Gathas*.[28]

The Zoroastrian description of final events will be familiar to anyone acquainted with Judaeo-Christian traditions. The Hebraic image of a Messianic Age, when the earth would flower in abundance and a holy people would reign in Palestine in peace and justice, is remarkably similar to the Zoroastrian *fraso-kereti*. The Christian belief in the gradual spiritual perfection of mankind, "an immanent process that would in time culminate in a golden age of happiness on earth, a millennium with the returned Christ as ruler," [162] could stand unchanged, but for the name of the saviour, as Zoroastrian doctrine. If Zarathustra did live in the seventh millennium, the idea that the world and mankind are moving toward a final state of perfection—that time is linear rather than cyclical—would presumably be equally old, and its revelation may represent the beginning of the split between western and oriental experiences of time.

The concept that we are progressing toward a better future is considered to be one of the most powerful forces in the shaping of Western civilization, and has consistently been linked with religion or intellectual constructs derived from religion.[162] Although the Judaeo-Christian worldview is most often cited as fundamental to the development of the idea of progress, it is actually in the Zoroastrian religion that the concept of a future paradise *on earth* may be said to have realized its "fullest logical coherence."[27] For it was Zarathustra who most clearly emphasized the goodness of the material world.

While the Christian tradition is essentially centered on man, for whose use the natural world seems to have been created, the Zoroastrian religion sees every element of the Good Creation as infused with spirit, striving "consciously or unconsciously to reach the one glorious goal of Fraso-kereti."[28] The follower of Zoroastrian principles understands that he is advancing his own moral and spiritual condition—perfecting himself—by helping all of the earthly domains reach that ultimate goal. It is this belief in the divinity and interconnectedness of every aspect of the material world—and in man's responsibility with regard to the other creations—that encourages a comparison of the teachings of Zarathustra with another largely unrecognized influence on the course of Western civilization: the alchemical tradition.

The Alchemical Heritage

We have noted Zarathustra's apparent interest in accurate and useful *page 121* knowledge of the material world, what we today would call natural science. It may not be coincidental, therefore, that one of the forerunners of modern science, the much misunderstood practice of alchemy, was based on a committment to the perfecting of both man and nature that strikingly resembles the Zoroastrian ideal. Popularly identified today with attempts in the Middle Ages to turn lead "magically" into gold, alchemy was actually a great deal older and directed toward a more profound goal: in the words of a medieval alchemist, "how Nature may be seen and recognized as coming from God, and God in Nature."[65] For the alchemist, not only man but all of nature's kingdoms—mineral as well as plant and animal—were moving toward an ultimate state of perfection, a "maturation" which the alchemist, through his ability to transmute material substance, was able to assist. It is a worldview which, along with the description of the alchemist as "the brotherly saviour of Nature,"[65] seems almost indistinguishable from the teachings of Zarathustra.

In his acclaimed study, *The Forge and the Crucible*, Mircea Eliade observed that alchemy "prolongs and consummates a very old dream of *homo faber*: collaboration in the perfecting of matter while at the same time securing perfection for himself."[65] The origin of that very old dream is unknown; writings of the alchemists say only that they built on what went before, on a divinely inspired tradition of great age.[23] Some scholars find the beginnings of alchemy in the Hermetic schools of Egypt in the second and third century AD, but others see Hellenistic Egypt as merely the inheritor of a body of knowledge that had long been incubating in Mesopotamia under the influence of the Magi.* If the alchemical worldview can indeed be traced to the Magi —and if ancestors of these archetypal "masters of fire" were already disseminating Zarathustra's teachings in the seventh and sixth millennia —what has come down to us as the alchemical tradition may actually be as old as the earliest transformation of the mineral realm, the beginning of metallurgy itself.

---

*In ancient texts it was "Ostanes the Magus" who taught Democritus the art of alchemy,[70] and in cuneiform tablets from seventh century BC Nineveh, a prescription for the ritual construction of a furnace for minerals refers to the ores as "embryos," a favorite alchemical analogy based on the idea that the fire of the furnace assists in the perfecting, or the maturing, of mineral substance. A comparable document from Hellenistic Egypt has convinced some investigators that Egyptian alchemy was rooted in Babylonian practices of far greater age.[64, 186]

In the sixteenth and seventeenth centuries AD, the alchemical interest in the transmutation of metals began gradually to merge with what was to become modern chemistry. The Swiss alchemist and physician Paracelsus (1493-1541) had studied both metallurgy and the traditions of the Magi, and it was through his work that alchemy began to be associated with the earliest forms of medical chemistry. Robert Boyle (1627-91), often referred to as the father of modern chemistry, was actually as much an alchemist, at least in its mundane form, as he was a chemist. And Issac Newton (1642-1727), whom some consider to have been the greatest of all scientists, is known to have spent many hours in his laboratory at Cambridge in the experimental pursuit of an alchemical wisdom whose spiritual dimension was an integral part of the work.[125]

Since that time alchemy has been overwhelmed (and ultimately scorned) by modern science, but its principles are still recognizable in the progress-centered ideologies of the modern age. Eliade found the alchemical tradition, stripped of its spiritual content, carried forward by the progress of industrialization and the experimental sciences:

> "It is in the specific dogma of the nineteenth century, according to which man's true mission is to transform and improve upon Nature and become her master, that we must look for the authentic continuation of the alchemist's dream. The visionary's myth of the perfection, or more accurately, of the redemption of Nature, survives, in camouflaged form, in the pathetic program of the industrial societies whose aim is the total transmutation of Nature, its transformation into "energy."[65]

Eliade's perception illustrates the fate of the progress-centered worldview when it becomes dislodged from its spiritual context. One need not believe in the interconnectedness of all life to recognize the degree to which man's exploitation of the other realms of nature has diminished his own experience of life on earth. The effects of our willful "dominion" over nature have been exaggerated by an immense growth in population and the urbanizing of human culture. Theoretically, both of these latter phenomena may be traced back to the time when the agricultural way of life began to spread irreversibly across Europe and

Asia—the time we have proposed here for Zarathustra. Does this mean that the overcrowded, industrialized, urban centers of today are to be his ultimate legacy?

The Ecology of an Animate World

The spread of farming that we have described in this book seems everywhere to have been accompanied by increases in population, technological advances, and, ultimately, the development of cities. Archaeologists working in southwestern Iran have concluded that the mid-to-late seventh millennum transition to settled farming set certain peoples there and in Mesopotamia "clearly on the path toward population expansion and urban life."[104] This path would lead to Susa, Babylon, and ultimately to sprawling cities like modern Tehran, whose suburbs have now expanded to engulf the ancient mound of Cheshmeh Ali.[138]

Few prehistorians living in today's all too well-populated and urbanized world see this irrevocable final phase of the Neolithic Revolution as an unmixed blessing. It is true that the development of agriculture forms the necessary basis for the development of great civilizations; surplus food enables a considerable part of the population to turn to new, and arguably more creative, occupations. But it is also true that modern industrial civilization, "the empire of cities that now holds the entire planet in its grip,"[193] is eating away at the substance of the earth and discharging pollutants into the air, the waters, even the earth itself. The destruction of the natural world seems a very high price for what we in the West once hailed unquestioningly as the progress of human culture.

But if both the belief in progress and the irreversible spread of agriculture can ultimately be traced to the seventh millennium teachings of Zarathustra, so too can the idea of man's responsible stewardship of the earth, the only lasting solution, perhaps, to the modern dilemma. The growing interest in ecology in the west could be an indication that the concept of stewardship, long dormant, is again on the rise. In attempting to reclaim overgrazed or industrially depleted earth, rescue threatened species of wildlife or animals abused in confinement, preserve the forests and restore the purity of the earth's waters, late twentieth and early twenty-first century men and women have become increasingly active — and through science, increasingly effective — in defending the Good Creation. In so doing, they may share in the legacy of a Neolithic prophet.

Others believe, however, that environmental conservation as practiced today will not be sufficient to break the habit of exploitation.[193] They argue that it is our fundamental relationship to the natural world that must be changed, and that this relationship will be healed only when human beings have learned — or relearned — to experience the earth as animate, alive. Not only Zarathustra and the alchemists, but virtually all traditional peoples envisioned an earth that was vitalized by unseen forces. For Plato as well, the world was a living being with intelligence in soul and soul "woven right through from the center to the outermost heaven." (*Timaeus* 36) Modern science has exchanged this "primitive" view of a living earth for a world composed of dead matter, but late in the twentieth century a more advanced level of scientific inquiry began questioning the wisdom of that exchange. Scientists working in several different fields of research began building theories in which the world was conceived to be not only alive but creative and even intentional.[193] The British biologist Rupert Sheldrake has in fact described his theory of morphic resonance as an "updated version of premechanistic animism."[203a]

Other well-known examples of this incremental shift of perspective within the scientific community include Gregory Bateson's work with the existence of Mind on all levels of sufficiently complex natural phenomena,[19] the physicist David Bohm's theory of an "implicate order" out of which everything (all seemingly separate entities) arises,[25b] and the astmospheric scientist James Lovelock's Gaia hypothesis, in which the earth itself is seen as a metabiological system capable of regulating the conditions necessary for all terrestrial life.[129a] Surveying these and related theories, the cultural historian Theodore Roszak observes that "the deeper modern science delves into the nature of things, the more it finds hints and traces of the primordial animist world." Roszak believes that in time this body of fact and theory may mature into an ecologically based form of animism, and "we will find ourselves once again on speaking terms with nature."[193]

"May we be those who will renew this existence."

page 68 This Gathic utterance (Y. 30.9) has received many translations over the years (e.g., "may we be those who make existence brilliant," "may we be those who shall transfigure this world"). Some interpreters see this passage as an indication that Zarathustra and his followers believed that the end of the world was imminent, that the *fraso-kereti* would be realized in their own lifetime. Whether or not that is an accurate interpretation of the Gathic hymn, the archaeological record suggests that a wide-ranging renewal was indeed underway in the last half of the seventh millenium BC. What happened between 6500 and 6000 BC was in every sense a reformation of human culture, and there are several indications that this cultural renewal included a rethinking of man's relationship to the natural world.

page 24 We have observed the possibility that depleted soils and forests around some of the larger PPNB settlements may have contributed to the early seventh millennium decline of PPNB culture and the abandonment of many of its long-standing sites. The overblown opulence of the huge PPNB-related settlement at Çatal Höyük added to the impression of an exhausted tradition. Comparing these signs of cultural decline to the description of the more numerous, but much smaller and more modest, painted pottery communities that sprang up after c. 6500 BC suggests that reducing the scale of man's collected presence on the earth might have been part of a conscious effort to restore the integrity of the natural world. The spread of irrigation techniques, which allowed

page 71 arid land ("ground that is dry") to be cultivated, would also have served to replenish the earth's capacity to sustain life. The theorized rescue of cattle from the abuses implied by the abundance of bulls' horns in the Çatal chambers, which were then present only in symbolic form among

page 50 the painted pottery communities, could represent a restructuring of man's relationship to the animal realm as well. If these were indeed accomplishments of Zarathustra's followers, the questions he poses to Ahura Mazda in the *Vendidad III* — "where does the earth feel most

page 57 happy?" "who gladdens the earth with greatest joy?" — indicate that the well-being of the earth, if not its profound renewal, was of primary concern to these late-seventh millennium farmers.

Service to the earth may in turn have affected their own well-being. To be glad and rejoice, to exuberantly celebrate the sanctity of the Good Creation, is a distinctly Zoroastrian trait. Feasting, music, merrymaking — "the utmost joyfulness" — has traditionally characterized the chain of festivals held throughout the year in honor of the Amesha Spentas, the divine emanations of Ahura Mazda that are believed to dwell within each of the earthly creations.[28] The vitality of late-seventh and sixth millennium painted pottery suggests that a similar exuberance may have prevailed in the farming villages of that epoch. With Armaiti, the spirit of the earth, perceived to be watching over farmers and herdsmen, life in these small agricultural communities would have been lived with a richness and depth of meaning that are, for us, unimaginable.

By contrast, the agribusinesses of today are particularly joyless industries whose goal seems to be the replacement of the world's agricultural diversity with patented, bioengineered monocultures that profit only the corporations.[24] But here again we find a countering force for renewal. In a recent interview, the small-farm activist Michael Abelman spoke of a new agricultural revolution in which workers on small-scale community farms are blending the wisdom of traditional agriculture with today's innovative technologies. He sees this new generation of farmers as artisans, creating a way of farming that restores its integrity as "an honorable profession, an art, a craft." For Abelman, a farm is not a factory but a living organism, and the men and women on these small farms work the land in a way that satisfies the needs of the earth as well as those of the marketplace. "To farm well," he tells us, "you have to merge with the biological world, which has inherent spiritual value."[1]

Like the environmentalists and theoretical scientists mentioned earlier, the small-farm activists are engaged in a struggle between two opposing ways of relating to the earth. And although we are separated, according to the perspective taken in this book, by more than eight thousand years from the struggle between two opposing forces that characterized Zarathustra's time, the outcome now as then will be determined by individual human choice. In the last half of the seventh millennium BC, thousands of hunter-gatherers, joined perhaps by groups of nomadic herdsmen, chose to give up their mobile ways of life, form permanent settlements, and cultivate the earth. In our interpretation, these newly converted farmers were consciously following the way of *asha* (truth, right order), which placed man in the role of steward, "husband," of the earth.

It has fairly been said that those who made that choice in the late seventh millennium BC shaped the future of human civilization. It seems no less fair to assume that the choices made by individuals living in the early third millenium AD will have an even greater impact, not only on the course of civilization but on the future life of the planet. To discover, or rediscover, the right relationship between man and the natural world is perhaps the most critical challenge of our time, one that is fundamental to all possibilities of renewal. Choosing to meet that challenge, joyfully, "each one for each," honors both the legacy of Zarathustra and the living earth for which he spoke.

Bibliography

1 Abelman, Michael, 2003. "Earthly Delights: Cultivating a New Agricultural Revolution," *The Sun*, 330: 4-14.

2 Adams, Jonathan and Marcel Otte, 1999. "Did Indo-European Languages Spread Before Farming?" *Current Anthropology* 40/1: 73-77.

3 Aguilar i Matas, E, 1991. *Rgvedic Society*, New York: E. J. Brill.

4 Akkermans, Peter M. M. G., 1993. *Villages in the Steppe*, Ann Arbor: International Monographs in Prehistory.

5 Akkermans, Peter M. M. G., 1996. *Tell Sabi Abyad*, Istanbul: Nederlands Historisch-Archaeologisch Institut.

6 Akkermans, Peter M. M. G. and Glenn M. Schwartz, 2003. *The Archaeology of Syria*, Cambridge: Cambridge University Press.

7 Ammerman, A. J. and L. L. Cavalli-Sforza, 1984. *The Neolithic Transition and the Genetics of Population in Europe*, Princeton: Princeton University Press.

8 Anthony, David W., 1995. "Horse, wagon, and chariot: Indo-European languages and archaeology," *Antiquity* 69: 554-65.

9 Bader, N. O., 1993a. "Tell Maghzaliyah: An Early Neolithic Site in Northern Iraq," in Norman Yoffee and Jeffery J. Clark, eds., *Early Stages in the Evolution of Mesopotamian Civilization*, Tucson: The University of Arizona Press.

10 Bader, N. O., 1993b. "The Early Agricultural Settlement of Tell Sotto," in Norman Yoffee and Jeffery J. Clark, eds., *Early Stages in the Evolution of Mesopotamian Civilization*, Tucson: The University of Arizona Press.

11 Bader, N. O., 1993c. "Summary of the Earliest Agriculturalists of Northern Mesopotamia (1989)," in Norman Yoffee and Jeffery J. Clark, eds., *Early Stages in the Evolution of Mesopotamian Civilization*, Tucson: The University of Arizona Press.

12 Bailey, Douglass W., 2000. *Balkan Prehistory*, London: Routledge.

13 Barker, Graeme, 1985. *Prehistoric Farming in Europe*, Cambridge: Cambridge University Press.

14 Bartholomae, Christian, 1961. *Altiranisches Wörterbuch*, Berlin: Walter de Gruyter (reprinted from 1904).

15 Bar-Yosef, Ofer, 1986. "The Walls of Jericho: an alternative interpretation," *Current Anthropology* 27/2: 157-62.

16 Bar-Yosef, Ofer, 1996. "The Impact of Late Pleistocene-Early Holocene Climatic Changes on Humans in Southwest Asia," in Lawrence Guy Straus et al, eds., *Humans at the End of the Ice Age*, New York: Plenum Press.

17 Bar-Yosef, Ofer, 2001. "PPNB Interaction Sphere," Review Feature, *Cambridge Archaeological Journal* ll/1: 114-17.

18 Bar-Yosef, Ofer, and Richard H. Meadow, 1995. "The Origins of Agriculture in the Near East," in T. Douglas Price and Anne Birgitte Gebauer, eds., *Last Hunters — First Farmers*, Santa Fe, New Mexico: School of American Research Press.

19 Bateson, Gregory, 1979. *Mind and Nature*, New York: E. P. Dutton

20 Beekes, Robert S. P., 1995. *Comparative Indo-European Linguistics*, Philadelphia: John Benjamins Publishing.

21 Belfer-Cohen, Anna, and Ofer Bar-Yosef, 2000. "Early Sedentism in the Near East," in Ian Kuijt, ed., *Life in Neolithic Farming Communities*, New York: Kluwer Academic/Plenum Publishers.

22 Benveniste, Emile, 1938. *Les Mages dans l'ancien Iran*, Paris: Adrien Maisonneuve.

23 Bernoulli, R., 1960. "Spiritual Development as Reflected in Alchemy and Related Disciplines." *Spiritual Disciplines. Papers from the Eranos Yearbook*, Zurich: Rhein-Verlag.

24 Berry, Wendell, 2003. *Citizenship Papers*, Washington DC: Shoemaker & Hoard.

25a Blinkenberg, Christopher, 1987. *The Thunderweapon in Religion and Folklore*, Cambridge: Cambridge University Press (reprinted from 1911).

25b Bohm, David, 1983. *Wholeness and the Implicate Order*, London: Routledge.

26 Boyce, Mary, 1975/1982. *A History of Zoroastrianism*, Vol. I/2, Leiden: E. J. Brill.

27 Boyce, Mary, 1979. *Zoroastrians, Their Religious Beliefs and Practices*, London: Routledge and Kegan Paul Ltd.

28 Boyce, Mary, 1992. *Zoroastrianism: Its Antiquity and Constant Vigor*, Costa Mesa, California: Mazda Publishers.

29 Boyce, Mary, ed., 1984. *Textual Sources for the Study of Zoroastrianism*, Totowa, New Jersey: Barnes & Noble Books.

30 Braidwood, Robert J., 1976. "The Background for Sumerian Civilization in the Euphrates-Tigris-Karun Drainage Basin" in D. Schmandt-Besserat, ed., *The Legacy of Sumer*, Malibu.

31 Braidwood, Robert J. et al, 1944. "New Chalcolithic Material of Samarran Type and Its Implications," *Journal of Near Eastern Studies* 3: 47-72.

32 Broodbank, Cyprian and Thomas F. Strasser, 1991. "Migrant Farmers and the Neolithic Colonization of Crete," *Antiquity* 65: 233-45.

33 Bryant, Edwin, 2001. *The Quest for the Origins of Vedic Culture*, New York: Oxford University Press.

34 Burney, C. A., 1964. "The Excavations at Yanik Tepe, Azerbaijan, 1962: Third Preliminary Report," *Iraq* 26: 54-61.

35 Campanile, Enrico, 1998. "The Indo-Europeans: Origins and Culture," in Anna Giacalone Ramat and Paolo Ramat, eds., *The Indo-European Languages*, New York: Routledge.

36 Caneva, Isabella, 1999. "Early Farmers on the Cilician Coast," in Mehmet Ozdogan and Nezih Basgelen, eds., *Neolithic in Turkey*. Istanbul: Arkeoloji ve Sanat Yayinlari.

37 Cauvin, Jacques, 2000a. *The Birth of the Gods and the Origins of Agriculture*, Trevor Watkins, trans., Cambridge: Cambridge University Press.

38 Cauvin, Jacques, 2000b. "The Symbolic Foundations of the Neolithic Revolution in the Near East," in Ian Kuijt, ed., *Life in Neolithic Farming Communities*, New York: Kluwer Academic/Plenum Publishers.

39 Cauvin, Jacques, 2001. "Ideology Before Economy," Review Feature, *Cambridge Archaeological Journal* 11/1: 106-107.

40 Cauvin, Marie-Claire, 1974. "Outillage lithique et chronologie à Tell Aswad." *Paléorient* 2/2: 429-36.

41 Cavalli-Sforza, L. Luca, 1996. "The spread of agriculture and nomadic pastoralism," in David R. Harris, ed., *The Origins and Spread of Agriculture and Pastoralism in Eurasia*, Washington, D. C.: Smithsonian Institution Press.

42 Cherry, J. F., 1990. "The First Colonization of the Mediterranean Islands," *Journal of Mediterranean Archaeology* 3/2: 145-221.

43 Chevalier, Jean, and Alain Gheerbrant, 1994. *A Dictionary of Symbols*, Oxford: Blackwell Publishers.

44 Cicero. *De republica* 3.14; *De legibus* 2.26.

45 Clark, Peter, 1998. *Zoroastrianism*, Portland, Oregon: Sussex Academic Press.

46 Cohn, Norman, 1993. *Cosmos, Chaos, and the World to Come*, London: Yale University Press.

47 Cook, A. B., 1914-40. *Zeus*, Vols. 1-III, Cambridge: Cambridge University Press.

48 Darmesteter, James (trans.), 1965. *The Zend-Avesta*, Vols. 1-II, Delhi: Motilal Banarsidass (reprinted from 1880).

49 de Jong, Albert, 1997. *Traditions of the Magi: Zoroastrianism in Greek and Latin Literature*, Leiden: Brill.

50 Delougaz, P. and H. J. Kantor, 1972. "New Evidence for the Prehistoric and Protoliterate Culture Development of Khuzistan," *Fifth Int'l Congress of Iranian Art and Archaeology, Tehran, 1968.*

51 Demoule, Jean-Paul, and Catherine Perlès, 1993. "The Greek Neolithic: A New Review," *Journal of World Prehistory*, Vol. 7, No. 4.

52 Deshpande, Madhav M., 1995. "Vedic Aryans, non-Vedic Aryans, and non-Aryans: Judging the linguistic evidence of the Veda," in George Erdosy, ed., *The Indo-Aryans of Ancient South Asia*, New York: Walter de Gruyter.

53 Dhalla, Viraf Minocher, 1994. *Symbols in Zoroastrianism*, Bombay: K. R. Cama Oriental Institute.

54 Diakonoff, Igor M., 1990. "Language Contacts in the Caucasus and the Near East," in T. L. Markey and John A. C. Greppin, eds., *When Worlds Collide*, Ann Arbor, Michigan: Karoma Publishers.

55 Diamond, Jared and Peter Bellwood, 2003. "Farmers and Their Languages: The First Expansions," *Science*, Vol. 300, April 25: 597-603.

56 Dicks, Brian, 1979. *The Ancient Persians*, London: David and Charles.

57 Diogenes Laertius. *Lives of Eminent Philosophers* I.2

58 Dolukhanov, P. M., 1986. "Foragers and farmers in west-Central Asia," in Marek Zvelebil, ed., *Hunters in Transition*, Cambridge: Cambridge University Press.

59 Duchesne-Guillemin, Jacques, 1958. *The Western Response to Zoroaster*, Westport, Connecticut: Greenwood Press.

60 Duchesne-Guillemin, Jacques, 1959. "Iranian Religion," in *Religions of the Ancient East*, New York: Hawthorn Books.

61 Dumezil, G., 1970. *The Destiny of the Warrior*, Chicago: University of Chicago Press

62 Dunand, M., 1973. "L'architecture, les tombes, le matériel domestique des origines néolithiques a l'avènement urbain," in *Fouilles de Byblos* 5, Paris: Librairie d'Amerique et d'Orient Jean Maisonneuve.

63 Dyson, Robert H., 1992. "Ceramics I. The Neolithic Period Through the Bronze Age in Northeastern and North-Central Persia," in Ehsan Yarshater, ed., *Encyclopaedia Iranica*, V, Costa Mesa, California: Mazda Publishers.

64 Eisler, R., 1926. "L'origine babylonienne de l'alchimie," *Revue de Synthése Historique* 25: 5-25.

65 Eliade, Mircea, 1971. *The Forge and the Crucible: The Origins and Structures of Alchemy*, New York: Harper and Row.

66 Eliade, Mircea, 1978. *A History of Religious Ideas*, Vol. 1, Chicago: The University of Chicago Press.

67 Esin, Ufuk, 1999. "Asikli," in Mehmet Ozdogan and Nezih Basgelen, eds., *Neolithic in Turkey*, Istanbul: Arkeoloji ve Sanat Yayinlari.

68 Fagan, Brian M. 1998. *People of the Earth*, New York: Longman.

69 Finkelberg, Margalit, 1997. "Anatolian Languages and the Indo-European Migrations to Greece," *Classical World* 91: 3-20.

70 Forbes, R. J., 1955. "The Origin of Alchemy," *in Studies in Ancient Technology I*, Leiden: Brill.

71 Frye, Richard N., 1996. *The Heritage of Central Asia*, Princeton: Markus Wiener.

72 Gamkrelidze, Thomas V., 1990. "On the Problem of an Asiatic Original Homeland of the Proto-Indo-Europeans," in T. L. Markey and John A. C. Greppin, eds., *When Worlds Collide*, Ann Arbor, Michigan: Karoma Publishers.

73 Gamkrelidze, T. V. and V. V. Ivanov, 1985. "The Ancient Near East and the Indo-European Question," *Journal of Indo-European Studies* 13: 3-91.

74 Gamkrelidze, T. V. and V. V. Ivanov, 1995. *Indo-European and the Indo-Europeans*, Vol. I, New York: Mouton de Gruyter.

75 Garrod, D. A. E., 1957. *The Natufian Culture*. London.

76 Geiger, Wilhelm, 1885. *Civilization of the Eastern Iranians in Ancient Times*, London: Oxford University Press.

77 Gershevitch, Ilya, 1964. "Zoroaster's Own Contribution," *Journal of Near Eastern Studies* 23: 12-38.

78 Gershevitch, Ilya, 1995. "Approaches to Zoroaster's Gathas," *Iran* 33: 1-30.

79 Ghirshman, Roman, 1938. *Fouilles de Tepe Sialk*, Vol. 1, Paris: Librairie Orientaliste Paul Geuthner.

80 Gimbutas, Marija, 1977. "The first wave of Eurasian steppe pastoralists into Copper Age Europe," *Journal of Indo-European Studies* 5: 277-338.

81 Gimbutas, Marija, 1988. Review of Colin Renfrew's *Archaeology and Language* in *Current Anthropology*, 29/3: 453-456.

82 Gimbutas, Marija, 1991. *The Civilization of the Goddess*. New York: HarperCollins.

83 Gimbutas, Marija, Shan Winn, Daniel Shimabuku, 1989. *Achilleion: A Neolithic Settlement in Thessaly, Greece, 6400-5600 BC*, Los Angeles: Regents of the University of California.

84 Glumac, Peter and David Anthony, 1992. "Culture and Environment in the Prehistoric Caucasus," in Robert W. Ehrich, ed., *Chronologies in Old World Archaeology*, Chicago: The University of Chicago Press.

85 Goff, B. L., 1963. *Symbols of Prehistoric Mesopotamia*, New Haven: Yale University Press.

86 Gopher, Avi, and Ram Gophna, 1993. "Cultures of the Eighth and Seventh Millennia BP in the Southern Levant," *Journal of World Prehistory*, 7/3: 297-353.

87 Goring-Morris, Nigel, 2000. "The Quick and the Dead," in Ian Kuijt, ed., *Life in Neolithic Farming Communities*, New York: Kluwer Academic/ Plenum Publishers.

88 Haarmann, Harald, 1998. "On the Problem of Primary and Secondary Diffusion of Indo-Europeans and Their Languages," *Journal of Indo-European Studies* 26: 391-419.

89 Halstead, Paul, 1996. "The development of agriculture and pastoralism in Greece: when, how, who and what?" in David R. Harris, ed., *The Origins and Spread of Agriculture and Pastoralism in Eurasia*, Washington, D. C.: Smithsonian Institution Press.

90 Harlan, Jack R., 1995. *The Living Fields.* Cambridge: Cambridge University Press.

91 Harris, David R., 1996. "The origins and spread of agriculture and pastoralism in Eurasia: an overview," in David R. Harris, ed., *The Origins and Spread of Agriculture and Pastoralism in Eurasia*, Washington, D. C.: Smithsonian Institution Press,

92 Harris, David. R., 1998. "The Spread of Neolithic Agriculture from the Levant to Western Central Asia," in A. B. Damania, J. Valkoun, G. Willcox, and C. O. Qualset, eds., *The Origins of Agriculture and Crop Domestication*, International Center for Agricultural Research in the Dry Areas.

93 Harris, David R. and Chris Gosden, 1996. "The beginnings of agriculture in western Central Asia," in David R. Harris, ed., *The Origins and Spread of Agriculture and Pastoralism in Eurasia*, Washington, D. C.: Smithsonian Institution Press.

94 Harris, D. R., C. Godsen, M. P. Charles. 1996. "Jeitun," *Proccedings of the Prehistoric Society* 62: 423-442.

95 Hayden, Brian, 1995. "A New Overview of Domestication," in T. Douglas Price and Anne Birgitte Gebauer, eds., *Last Hunters – First Farmers*, Santa Fe, New Mexico: School of American Research Press.

96 Herzfeld, E. E., 1947. *Zoroaster and His World.* Princeton: Princeton University Press.

97 Hiebert, Fredrik T., 1998. "Central Asians on the Iranian Plateau," in Victor H. Mair, ed., *The Bronze Age and Early Iron Age Peoples of Eastern Central Asia.* Washington DC: Institute for the Study of Man Inc.

98 Hillman, Gordon, 2003. "Investigating the Start of Cultivation in Western Eurasia," in Albert J. Ammerman and Paolo Biagi, eds., *The Widening Harvest,* Boston: Archaeological Institute of America.

99 Hodder, Ian, 1989. *The Meanings of Things: Material Culture and Symbolic Expression,* London: Unwin and Hyman.

100 Hodder, Ian, 1999. "Renewed Work at Çatalhöyük" in Mehmet Ozdogan and Nezih Basgelen, eds., *Neolithic in Turkey,* Istanbul: Arkeoloji ve Sanat Yayinlari.

101 Hodder, Ian, 2004. Personal communication.

102 Hole, Frank, 1987. "Archaeology of the Village Period," in Frank Hole, ed., *The Archaeology of Western Iran,* Washington DC: Smithsonian Institution Press.

103 Hole, Frank, 2000. "Is Size Important?" in Ian Kuijt, ed., *Life in Neolithic Farming Communities,* New York: Kluwer Academic/Plenum Publishers.

104 Hole, Frank and Kent V. Flannery, 1967. "The Prehistory of Southwestern Iran," *Proceedings of the Prehistoric Society* 33: 147-206.

105a Humbach, Helmut, 1984. "A Western Approach to Zarathushtra," *Journal of the K. R. Cama Oriental Institute* 51.

105b Humbach, Helmut, 1991. *The Gathas of Zarathustra,* Heidelberg: Carl Winter Universitätsverlag.

106 Huot, Jean-Louis, 1965. *Persia I: From the Origins to the Achaemenids,* Geneva, Switzerland: Nagle.

107 Insler, S., 1975. *The Gathas of Zarathustra,* Acta Iranica 8, Leiden: E. J. Brill.

108 Jackson, A. V. W., 1928. *Zoroastrian Studies,* New York: Columbia University Press.

109 Jacobsen, T. W., 1981. "Franchthi Cave and the Beginning of Settled Village Life in Greece," *Hesperia* 50: 303-19.

110 Jarrige, Jean-Francois, 1993. "Excavations at Mehrgarh," in Gregory Possehl, ed., *Harappan Civilization,* New Delhi: American Institute of Indian Studies.

111 Kellens, Jean, 2000. *Essays on Zarathustra and Zoroastrianism,* Costa Mesa, California: Mazda Publishers.

112 Kenyon, Kathleen, 1957. *Digging Up Jericho.* London: E. Benn.

113 Kenyon, Kathleen, 1960. "Excavations at Jericho, 1957-58," *Palestine Excavation Quarterly*, 1-21.

114 Kingsley, Peter, 1995. "Meetings with Magi: Iranian Themes Among the Greeks, from Xanthus of Lydia to Plato's Academy," *Journal of the Royal Asiatic Society* 5/2: 173-210.

115 Kirkbride, Diana, 1968. "Beidha: Early Neolithic Village Life South of the Dead Sea," *Antiquity* 42: 263-74.

116 Kohl, Philip L., 1992. "Central Asia: Neolithic to the Early Iron Age," in Robert W. Ehrich, ed., *Chronologies in Old World Archaeology*, Chicago: The University of Chicago Press.

117 Kohler-Rollefson, I. and G. O. Rollefson, 1990. "The Impact of Neolithic Subsistence Strategies on the Environment," in S. Bottema, G. Entjes-Nieborg, and W. van Zeist, eds., *Man's Role in the Shaping of the Eastern Mediterranean Landscape*, Rotterdam: A. A. Balkema.

118 Kozlowski, S. K., 1999. *The Eastern Wing of the Fertile Crescent*, BAR International Series 760, Oxford: Archaeopress.

119 Kriwaczek, Paul, 2003. *In Search of Zarathustra*, New York: Alfred A. Knopf.

120 Kuijt, Ian, 2000. "Introduction." in Ian Kuijt, ed., *Life in Neolithic Farming Communities*, New York: Kluwer Academic/Plenum Publishers.

121 Kuzmina, E. E., 2001. "The First Migration Wave of Indo-Iranians to the South," *The Journal of Indo-European Studies* 29: 1-40.

122 Lamberg-Karlovsky, C. C., 2002. "Archaeology and Language," *Current Anthropology* 43/1: 63-88.

123 Lazzeroni, Romano, 1998. "Sanskrit," in Anna Giacalone Ramat and Paolo Ramat, eds., *The Indo-European Languages*, New York: Routledge.

124 Leblanc, Steven. A. and Patty Jo Watson, 1973. "A Comparative Statistical Analysis of Painted Pottery from Seven Halafian Sites," *Paleorient* I: 117-33

125 Levere, Trevor, 2001. *Transforming Matter: A History of Chemistry from Alchemy to the Buckyball*, London: The Johns Hopkins University Press.

126 Lincoln, Bruce, 1981. *Priests, Warriors, and Cattle*, Berkeley: University of California Press.

127 Lisitsina, G. N., 1984. "The Caucasus – a center of ancient farming in Eurasia," in W. Van Zeist and W. A. Casparie, eds., *Plants and Ancient Man*, Rotterdam: A. A. Balkema.

128 Lloyd, S. and F. Safar, 1945. "Tell Hassuna," *Journal of Near Eastern Studies* 4: 255-89.

129a Lovelock, James, 1979. *Gaia: A New Look at Life on Earth*, New York: Oxford University Press.

129b Majidzadeh, Y., 1979. "An Early Prehistoric Coppersmith Workshop at Tepe Ghabristan," *Archaeologische Mitteilungen aus Iran* 6: 82-92.

130 Malandra, William W., 1983. *An Introduction to Ancient Iranian Religion*, Minneapolis: University of Minnesota Press.

131 Maleki, Yolande, 1968. "Abstract Art and Animal Motifs Among the Ceramics of the Region of Tehran," *Archaeologica Viva* 1: 42-50

132 Mallory, James P., 1989. *In Search of the Indo-Europeans*, London: Thames and Hudson.

133 Mallory, James P., 1997. "The Homelands of the Indo-Europeans," in Roger Blench and Matthew Spriggs, eds., *Archaeology and Language* I, New York: Routledge.

134 Mallory, James P., 1998. "A European Perspective on Indo-Europeans in Asia," in Victor H. Mair, ed., *The Bronze Age and Early Iron Age Peoples of Eastern Central Asia*, Washington DC: Institute for the Study of Man.

135 Mallowan, M. E. L., 1970. "The Development of Cities from Al-'Ubaid to the End of Uruk 5," in *Cambridge Ancient History* I. Cambridge: Cambridge University Press.

136 Mallowan, M. E. L. and J. C. Rose, 1935. "Excavations at Tell Arpachiyah 1933," *Iraq* 2: 1-178.

137 Masuda, S., 1974. "Excavations in Iran During 1972-73: Tepe Sang-e Caxamaq," *Iran* 12: 222-23.

138 Matney, Timothy, 1995. "Re-excavating Cheshmeh Ali," *Expedition* 37/2: 26-32.

139 Matyushin, G., 1986. "The Mesolithic and Neolithic in the southern Urals and Central Asia," in Marek Zvelebil, ed., *Hunters in Transition*, Cambridge: Cambridge University Press.

140 McCown, Donald E., 1942. "The Material Culture of Early Iran," *Journal of Near Eastern Studies* 1: 424-450.

141 Meadow, Richard H., 1996. "The origins and spread of agriculture and pastoralism in northwestern South Asia,"in David R. Harris, ed., *The Origins and Spread of Agriculture and Pastoralism in Eurasia*, Washington D. C.: Smithsonian Institution Press.

142 Mellaart, James, 1963. "Excavations at Çatal Hüyük: Second Preliminary Report," *Anatolian Studies* 13: 43-103.

143 Mellaart, James, 1964. "Excavations at Çatal Hüyük: Third Preliminary Report," *Anatolian Studies* 14: 39-119.

144 Mellaart, James, 1966. "Excavations at Çatal Hüyük: Fourth Preliminary Report," *Anatolian Studies* 16: 165-91.

145 Mellaart, James, 1967. *Çatal Hüyük, A Neolithic Town in Anatolia*, London: Thames and Hudson.

146 Mellaart, James. 1970. *Excavations at Hacilar*, Edinburgh: Edinburgh University Press.

147 Mellaart, James, 1975. *The Neolithic of the Near East*, London: Thames and Hudson.

148 Merpert, N. Ya., 1993. "The Archaic Phase of the Hassuna Culture," in Norman Yoffee and Jeffery J. Clark, eds., *Early Stages in the Evolution of Mesopotamian Civilization*, Tucson: The University of Arizona Press.

149 Merpert, N. Ya. and R. M. Munchaev, 1993a. "Yarim Tepe I: Upper Hassuna Levels," in Norman Yoffee and Jeffery J. Clark, eds., *Early Stages in the Evolution of Mesopotamian Civilization*, Tucson: The University of Arizona Press.

150 Merpert, N. Ya. and R. M. Munchaev, 1993b. "Yarim Tepe II: The Halaf Levels," in Norman Yoffee and Jeffery J. Clark, eds., *Early Stages in the Evolution of Mesopotamian Civilization*, Tucson: The University of Arizona Press.

151 Merpert, N. Ya. and R. M. Munchaev, 1993c. "The Earliest Evidence for Metallurgy in Ancient Mesopotamia," in Norman Yoffee and Jeffery J. Clark, eds., *Early Stages in the Evolution of Mesopotamian Civilization*, Tucson: The University of Arizona Press.

152 Mills, L. H., trans., 1965. *The Zend-Avesta*, Vol. III, Delhi: Motilal Banarsidass (reprinted from 1887).

153 Moore, A. M. T., 1989. "The transition from foraging to farming in Southwest Asia," in David R. Harris and Gordon C. Hillman, eds., *Foraging and Farming*, London: Unwin Hyman.

154 Moore, A. M. T., 1995. "The Inception of Potting in Western Asia and Its Impact on Economy and Society" in William K. Barnett and John W. Hoopes, eds., *The Emergence of Pottery*, Washington: Smithsonian Institution Press.

155 Moore, A. M. T., G. C. Hillman, A. J. Legge, 2000. *Village on the Euphrates*, New York: Oxford University Press.

156 Mortensen, Peder, 1992. "Ceramics II. The Neolithic Period in Central and Western Persia," in Ehsan Yarshater, ed., *Encyclopaedia Iranica V*, Costa Mesa, California: Mazda Publishers.

157 Munchaev, R. M., 1993. "Some Problems in the Archaeology of Mesopotamia in Light of Recent Research by the Soviet Expedition to Iraq," in Norman Yoffee and Jeffery J. Clark, eds., *Early Stages in the Evolution of Mesopotamian Civilization*, Tucson: The University of Arizona Press.

158 Negahban, E. O., 1979. "The Painted Building of Zaghe," *Paleorient* 5: 239-250.

159 Neuninger, H., R. Pittoni, and W. Siegel, 1969. "Frühkeramikzeitliche Kupfergewinnung in Anatolien," *Archaeologia Austriaca* 46: 98-110.

160 Nietzsche, Friedrich Wilhelm, 1883. *Also Sprach Zarathustra* (Thus Spake Zarathustra).

161 Nigosian, S. A., 1993. *The Zoroastrian Faith*, Montreal: McGill-Queen's University Press.

162 Nisbet, Robert, 1980. *History of the Idea of Progress*, New York: Basic Books.

163 Nyberg, H. S., 1966. *Die Religionen des Alten Iran*, Osnabrück: O. Zeller.

164 Oates, Joan, 1969. "Choga Mami, 1967-68: A Preliminary Report," *Iraq* 31: 115-52.

165 Oates, Joan, 1973. "The Background and the Development of Early Farming Communities in Mesopotamia and the Zagros," *Proceedings of the Prehistoric Society* 39: 147-81.

166 O'Flaherty, Wendy, 1981. *The Rig Veda*, New York: Penguin Books.

167 Otto, Brinna, 1985. *Die Verzierte Keramik der Sesklo- und Diminikultur Thessaliens*, Mainz am Rhein: Verlag Phillip von Zabern.

168 Özdogan, Asli, 1999. "Çayönü," in Mehmet Özdogan and Nezih Basgelen, eds., *Neolithic in Turkey*, Istanbul: Arkeoloji ve Sanat Yayinlari.

169 Özdogan, Mehmet, 1995. "Neolithic in Turkey" in *Readings in Prehistory. Studies Presented to Halet Cambel.* Istanbul: Graphis.

170 Özdogan, Mehmet, 1999. "Northwestern Turkey," in Mehmet Özdogan and Nezih Basgelen, eds., *Neolithic in Turkey*, Istanbul: Arkeoloji ve Sanat Yayinlari.

171 Özdogan, Mehmet and Asli Özdogan, 1998. "Buildings of Cult and the Cult of Buildings," in Güven Arsebük, Machteld J. Mellink, Wulf Schirmer, eds., *Light on the Top of the Black Hill*, Istanbul: Ege Yayinlari.

172 Özdogan, M. and I. Gatsov, 1998. "The Aceramic Neolithic Period in Western Turkey and the Aegean." *Anatolica* XXIV: 209-232.

173 Perlès, Catherine, 2001. *The Early Neolithic in Greece*, Cambridge: Cambridge University Press.

174 Perrot, J., 1952. "Têtes de flèches du Natoufien et du Tahounien (Palestine)," *Bulletin de la société prehistorique française* 49: 439-49.

175 Perrot, J., 1966. "Le gisement Natoufien de Mallaha (Eynan), Israel." *L'Anthropologie* 70: 437-83.

176 Phillips, P., 1975. *Early Farmers of West Mediterraneann Europe*, London.

177 Pliny, *Natural History* 30.3-4.

178 Plutarch, *De Iside et Osiride* 46.

179 Porada, Edith, 1969. *The Art of Ancient Iran*, New York: Greystone Press.

180 Porada, Edith, Donald P. Hansen, Sally Dunham, Sidney H. Babcock, 1992. "The Chronology of Mesopotamia, ca. 7000-1600 BC," in Robert W. Ehrich, ed., *Chronologies in Old World Archaeology*, Chicago: The University of Chicago Press.

181 Price, T. Douglas, 2000. "Lessons in the transition to agriculture," in T. Douglas Price, ed., *Europe's First Farmers*, Cambridge: Cambridge University Press.

182 Redman, Charles L., 1978. *The Rise of Civilization*, San Francisco: W. H. Freeman.

183 Renfrew, Colin, 1987. *Archaeology and Language: the puzzle of Indo-European origins*, New York: Cambridge University Press.

184 Renfrew, Colin, 1996. "Language families and the spread of farming," in David R. Harris, ed., *The Origins and Spread of Agriculture and Pastoralism in Eurasia*, Washington D. C.: Smithsonian Institution Press.

185 Renfrew, Colin, 1999. "Time Depth, Convergence Theory, and Innovation in Proto-Indo-European: 'Old Europe' as a PIE Linguistic Area," *The Journal of Indo-European Studies*, 27: 258-293.

186 Rey, A., 1930. *La science orientale avant les Grecs*, Paris.

187 Richards, M. R., H. Corte-Real, P. Forster, V. Macaulay, H. Wilkinson-Herbots, A. Demaine, S. Papiha, R. Hedges, H.-J. Bandelt, and B C. Sykes, 1996. "Paleolithic and Neolithic Lineages in the European Mitochondrial Gene Pool," *American Journal of Human Genetics* 59: 185-203.

188 Rodden, R. J., 1962. "Excavations at Nea Nikomedeia," *Proceedings of the Prehistoric Society* 27: 267-88.

189 Rollefson, Gary O., 1989. "The Collapse of Early Neolithic Settlements in the Southern Levant," in *People and Cultures in Change*, BAR International Series 508 (i).

190 Rollefson, Gary O., 2000. "Ritual and Social Structure at Neolithic 'Ain Ghazal," in Ian Kuijt, ed., *Life in Neolithic Farming Communities*. New York: Kluwer Academic/Plenum Publishers.

191 Roodenberg, J.- J., 1979-80. "Premiers résultats de recherches archéologiques à Hayaz Höyük," *Anatolica* 7: 3-19.

192 Rose, Jenny, 2000. *The Image of Zoroaster*, New York: Bibliotheca Persica Press.

193 Roszak, Theodore, 1992. *The Voice of the Earth*, New York: Simon and Schuster.

194 Roux, Georges, 1992. *Ancient Iraq*, London: Penguin Books Ltd.

195 Runnels, Curtis, and Priscilla Murray, 2001. *Greece Before History.* Stanford, California: Stanford University Press.

196 Sarianidi, V., 1992. "Food-producing and other Neolithic communities in Khorasan and Transoxania: east Iran, Soviet Central Asia and Afghanistan," in A. H. Dani and V. M. Masson, eds., *History of Civilizations of Central Asia*, Vol. 1, Paris: UNESCO.

197 Schmidt, Erich, 1935. "The Persian Expedition," *Bulletin of the Museum of the University of Pennsylvania* 5/5: 41-49.

198 Schmidt, K., 2001. "Göbekli Tepe, Southeastern Turkey," *Paleorient* 26/1: 45-54.

199 Shaked, Shaul, 2004. "The Yasna Ritual in Pahlavi Literature," in Michael Stausberg, ed., *Zoroastrian Rituals in Context*, Leiden: E. J. Brill.

200 Shaked, Shaul, 1984. "Iranian Influence on Judaism," in W. D. Davies and Louis Finkelstein, eds., *The Cambridge History of Judaism*, New York: Cambridge University Press.

201 Shaked, Shaul, 1995. *From Zoroastrian Iran to Islam*, Brookfield, Vermont: Ashgate Publishing Company.

202 Sharif, M. and B. K. Thapar, 1992. "Food-producing communities in Pakistan and northern India," in A. H. Dani and V. M. Masson, eds., *History of Civilizations of Central Asia*, Vol. 1, Paris: UNESCO.

203a Sheldrake, Rupert, 1981. *A New Science of Life*, Los Angeles: Jeremy Tarcher.

203b Sherratt, Andrew, 1988. Review of Colin Renfrew's *Archaeology and Language* in *Current Anthropology* 29/3: 458-463.

204 Simmons, Alan H., 2000. "Villages on the Edge," in Ian Kuijt, ed., *Life in Neolithic Farming Communities*, New York: Kluwer Academic/Plenum Publishers.

205 Sims-Williams, Nicholas, 1998. "The Iranian Languages," in Anna Giacalone Ramat and Paolo Ramat, eds., *The Indo-European Languages*, New York: Routledge.

206 Skjaervo, Prods Oktor, 1996. "Zarathustra in the Avesta and in Manicheism," *La Persia e l'Asia centrale da Alessandro...*, Rome.

207 Srinivasan, Doris, 1979. *Concept of Cow in the Rigveda*, Delhi: Motilal Banarsidass.

208 Stager, Lawrence E., 1992. "The Periodization of Palestine from Neolithic through Early Bronze Times," in Robert W. Ehrich, ed., *Chronologies in Old World Archaeology*, Chicago: The University of Chicago Press.

209 Stordeur, D., 2000. "New Discoveries in Architecture and Symbolism at Jerf el-Ahmar (Syria) 1997-1999," *Neo-Lithics* 1/00: 1-4.

210 Taraporewala, I. J. S., 1947. *The Gathas of Zarathustra*, Bombay.

211 Theocharis, D. R., 1973. *Neolithic Greece.* Athens: National Bank of Greece.

212 Thorpe, I. J., 1996. *The Origins of Agriculture in Europe*, London: Routledge.

213 Tosi, M., S. Malek Shahmirzadi, and M. A. Joyenda, 1992. "The Bronze Age in Iran and Afghanistan," in A. H. Dani and V. M. Masson, eds., *History of Civilizations of Central Asia*, Vol. 1, Paris: UNESCO.

214 Tringham, Ruth, 2000. "Southeastern Europe in the transition to agriculture in Europe: bridge, buffer, or mosaic," in T. Douglas Price, ed., *Europe's First Farmers*, Cambridge: Cambridge University Press.

215 Van Andel, T. H. and J. C. Shackelton, 1982. "Late Paleolithic and Mesolithic Coastlines of Greece and the Aegean," *Journal of Field Archaeology* 9: 445-54.

216 Van Den Berghe, L., 1968. "The Rich Naturalistic Influence in Iranian Painted Pottery," *Archaeologica Viva* I: 20-33

217 Vencl, Slavomil, 1986. "The role of hunting-gathering populations in the transition to farming," in Marek Zvelebil, ed., *Hunters in Transition*, Cambridge, England: Cambridge University Press.

218 Verhoeven, J., 2002. "Ritual and Ideology in the Pre-Pottery Neolithic B," *Cambridge Archaeological Journal* 12/2: 233-58.

219 Vitelli, Karen D., 1989. "Were pots first made for foods?" *World Archaeology* 21: 17-29.

220 Vitelli, Karen D., 1993. "Franchthi Neolihic Pottery," *Excavations at Franchthi Cave*, fasc. 8, Bloomington: Indiana University Press.

221 Vitelli, Karen D., 1995. "Pots, Potters, and the Shaping of Greek Neolithic Society" in William K. Barnett and John W. Hoopes, eds., *The Emergence of Pottery*, Washington DC: Smithsonian Institution Press.

222 Voigt, Mary M., 1983. *Hajii Firuz Tepe, Iran: The Neolithic Settlement*, Philadelphia: The University Museum.

223 Voigt, Mary M., 1992. "Ceramics I. The Neolithic Period in Northwestern Persia," in Ehsan Yarshater, ed., *Encyclopaedia Iranica* V, Costa Mesa, California: Mazda Publishers.

224 Voigt, Mary M., 2000. "Çatal Höyük in Context," in Ian Kuijt, ed., *Life in Neolithic Farming Communities*, New York: Kluwer Academic/Plenum Publishers.

225 Voigt, Mary M., 2004. Personal communication.

226 Voigt, Mary M. and Robert H. Dyson, Jr., 1992. "The Chronology of Iran, ca. 8000-2000 BC," in Robert W. Ehrich, ed., *Chronologies in Old World Archaeology,* Chicago: The University of Chicago Press.

227 Watkins, Calvert, 1998. "Proto Indo-European: Comparison and Reconstruction" in Anna Giacalone Ramat and Paolo Ramat, eds., *The Indo-European Languages,* New York: Routledge.

228 Watkins, Trevor, 1992. "The Beginning of the Neolithic," *Paleorient* 18/1: 63-75.

229 Watkins, Trevor, 1998. "The Human Environment," *Paleorient* 23/2: 263-270.

230 Watkins, Trevor, 2001. "Response," Review Feature, *Cambridge Archaeological Journal* 11/1: 117-119.

231 Watson, Patty Jo, and Steven A Leblanc, 1990. *Girikihaciyan: A Halafian Site in Southeastern Turkey,* Monograph 33, Institute of Archaeology, University of California, Los Angeles.

232 Webster, Charles, 1982. *From Paracelsus to Newton: Magic and the Making of Modern Science,* New York: Cambridge University Press.

233 Weinberg, S. S., 1961. "Halafian and 'Ubaidian Influence in Neolithic Greece." *5th International Congress of Prehistoric and Protohistoric Sciences, Hamburg, 1958,* Berlin.

234 Welburn, Andrew, 1991. *The Book with Fourteen Seals,* Sussex, England: Rudolf Steiner Press.

235 Whittle, Alasdair, 1996. *Europe in the Neolithic.* Cambridge: Cambridge University Press.

236 Williams, Ron G. and James W. Boyd, 1993. *Ritual Art and Knowledge: Aesthetic Theory and Zoroastrian Ritual,* Columbia, South Carolina: University of South Carolina Press.

237 Wood, Andree R., 1998. "Revisited: Blood Residue Investigations at Çayönü, Turkey," in Guven Arsebuk, Macteld J. Mellink, Wulf Schirmer, eds., *Light on Top of the Black Hill,* Istanbul: Ege Yayinlari.

238 Wright, Katherine I., 2000. "The Social Origins of Cooking and Dining in Early Villages of Western Asia," *Proceedings of the Prehistoric Society* 66: 89-121.

239 Yoffee, Norman, 1993. "Mesopotamian Interaction Spheres," in Norman Yoffee and Jeffery J. Clark, eds., *Early Stages in the Evolution of Mesopotamian Civilization,* Tucson: The University of Arizona Press.

240 York, Michael, 1995. *The Divine Versus the Asurian: An Interpretation of Indo-European Cult and Myth,* Bethesda, Maryland: International Scholars Publications.

241 Zaehner, R. C., 1961. *The Dawn and Twilight of Zoroastrianism*, New York: Putnam.

242 Zeder, Melinda A., 1994. "After the Revolution: Post-Neolithic Subsistence in Northern Mesopotamia," *American Anthropologist* 96/1: 97-126.

243 Zohary, Daniel, 1996. "The mode of domestication of the founder crops of Southwest Asian agriculture," in David R. Harris, ed., *The Origins and Spread of Agriculture and Pastoralism in Eurasia*, Washington D. C.: Smithsonian Institution Press.

244 Zohary, Daniel, and Maria Hopf, 2000. *Domestication of Plants in the Old World*, New York: Oxford University Press.

245 Zvelebil, Marek, and Kamil V. Zvelebil, 1988. "Agricultural transition and Indo-European dispersals," *Antiquity* 62: 574-83.

246 Zvelebil, Marek, and Malcolm Lillie, 2000. "Transition to agriculture in eastern Europe," in T. Douglas Price, ed., *Europe's First Farmers*, Cambridge: Cambridge University Press.

Index

Figure numbers of maps and illustrations appear in parentheses.

zarathustrotema 80-81
Zend-Avesta 53, 55, 69, 70, 126, 129
Zoroaster *(see* Zarathustra)
Zoroastrianism 53, 65, 109, 120, 125,
      126, 129
    dualism in, 10, 59-60, 74-75
    creation myth in, 59-60
    eschatology in, 61n, 67, 123n, 130